rendezvous

A SACRED ENCOUNTER WITH GOD

FRANK MOORE

BEACON HILL PRESS
OF KANSAS CITY

Copyright 2007
by Frank Moore and Beacon Hill Press of Kansas City

ISBN 978-0-8341-2297-0

Printed in the
United States of America

Cover Design: Brandon Hill
Internal Design: Sharon Page

All Scripture quotations not otherwise designated are from the *Holy Bible, New International Version*®
(NIV®). Copyright © 1973, 1978, 1984 by International Bible Society. Used by permission of Zonder-
van Publishing House. All rights reserved.

10 9 8 7 6 5 4 3 2 1

To my wife, Sue,
whose romance with God inspires me daily

CONTENTS

FOREWORD

This book is about passion—not the common use of the word, so often associated with mere human emotion. This book is about pursuing the central most important and consuming passion of your life. It is about romance, but it is about more than a momentary human encounter. This book is about building a life-altering relationship with your Beloved.

Following up on his outstanding and successful book, *The Power to Be Free,* Frank Moore has now given us guidance for cultivating a life of spiritual intimacy with the One who has set us free.

It was a gift of rare proportion for Dr. Moore to provide the previous book in the 40-day format. For the many people who had discovered that the Father desires to give us a purpose for living, the next most needed guidance was for a way to be free to live that life of purpose. The book quickly became one of the most widely published books in the history of Beacon Hill Press of Kansas City.

Nothing could be more necessary for those who have been encountered by the liberating Spirit than to know how to cultivate a life of such intimacy with Christ that they begin to take on His very character. That intimacy is not automatic, nor is it easy to accomplish. Even those whose hearts are pure must develop the disciplines and approaches to spiritual growth that will cultivate a deepening relationship with Jesus.

This journey may be very appropriately understood as a romance. It does not have to be drudgery or a task to be dreaded. It can be a much anticipated rendezvous. And Dr. Moore invites the reader into an experience in community, joining us with others who are pursuing the same intimacy with Christ we ourselves hunger to experience.

While you may with great profit read this book on your own, you will find the greatest benefit from joining with a group of other like-

7

minded seekers. A 40-day engagement with the guidance given by Dr. Moore will enable you and your sojourners to find strength and encouragement from one another as you engage in this sacred romance.

This is the book for which many have hoped. Here is help beyond a formulaic approach that leaves one frustrated with another set of demanding steps. This is life. This is relationship. This is an invitation to *Rendezvous!*

—Jesse C. Middendorf
General Superintendent, Church of the Nazarene
December 2006

A SACRED ENCOUNTER

They peer around the craggy walls, searching for each other. Strangers pass by, pausing to stare up at a crumbling parapet or look down at the murky water flowing far below. *Where is she?* he wonders. *Maybe he's not coming,* she thinks. The anxious thoughts come and go. Then they see it—a discreet gesture, a familiar turn of the head—it's her; it's him. Their hearts pound, their steps lighten, and suddenly they are hand-in-hand and face-to-face. Their long-awaited encounter has begun.

Manila's Fort Santiago is where Filipino lovers meet. It is where they go to escape family and friends, the customary escorts of their courtship. Here at this old Spanish fortress, an attraction for travelers and sightseers, a couple can steal away and openly speak their love and vow their devotion. They then all too quickly part, lingering for one last look, one final brush of the hand, before weaving their way down from where the old citadel is perched at the mouth of the river Pasig. They go back to their families, their jobs, and their friends, all the while waiting—yes, continually waiting—for their next time together, their next rendezvous.[1]

Wouldn't it be wonderful if we were just as entranced to meet with Christ? To have our hearts so captivated by Him that we could barely wait to be with Him for a few private moments together? And how marvelous would it be if on parting, we lingered in our prayers, longing for one more word from that "still small voice," one final caress from that all-caring hand? As we part our ways and go back to our schedules and responsibilities, we would think about the next time—the next time we would be together just like this!

If this excites you, if it makes your heart beat faster with the possibility of regularly rendezvousing with Christ, then I have good news! Not only is such an encounter possible, but Christ has designed ways and means of meeting with us as often as we like. In this book we will explore some of the many ways we can encounter Christ.

9

God creates us for fellowship with himself. He seeks to meet with us regularly. Rebellion against God set humanity running away from Him since the garden fall (see Gen. 3). Jesus Christ came to earth to bring us back to our Heavenly Father. When we answer God's call and end our rebellion, we allow Him to forgive us our sins so we can enter into a relationship with Him. And what a relationship it is! Daily communion with the Almighty Creator of the universe—nothing could be more satisfying than that.

We know this wonderful life with God is more than just discovering Christ, getting saved, and filing it all away. But isn't that what people sometimes do? They meet Christ in their early years and file Him away like an item checked off on a to-do list. When asked about their relationship with Christ, they respond, "Been there; done that." But have they? Have they really explored the depths of knowing Christ?

A genuine relationship with Christ is a consuming daily passion that should last a lifetime and beyond. It draws us back to Him through a variety of activities in a variety of settings with a variety of people. We cannot seem to quench our thirst for Him. The result of all this is a marvelous change in us. We become more like the One we love in character and conduct.

Christians sometimes wear wrist bracelets with the letters WWJD for What Would Jesus Do? Other believers search their Bibles regularly to find out how Jesus might respond in their particular situations. Still others pray for the Spirit of Christ to breathe a sense of direction into their lives. All of these exercises illustrate that Christians genuinely want to be more like Jesus.

One of the many benefits of spending time with Christ is developing a character like His. That's what this book will explore—becoming more like Jesus. But before we get too far ahead, let's keep this in mind: Christlike character is a by-product of a relationship with Him, not an isolated goal in itself. We encounter Christ throughout the daily events of our lives. Our desire to be with Him flows from our love for Him, not from the hope of a remade personality. Yet over time we do begin to look more and more like Jesus.

So this book will take us through basic practices that can be developed into an almost endless combination of settings, activities, and social groupings through which we encounter Christ. In Week 1 we'll explore ways Christ wants to relate with us. Weeks 2 to 6 will take a close look at ways we can encounter Christ by ourselves and with others.

Since we're using Christ as both our role model and example in this book, Scripture references for each day's readings will come from the four Gospels. Every Scripture focusing on the life and ministry of Jesus provides a pattern to apply to our lives. Too often we make the excuse of saying, "Jesus is God, so I'll never measure up to His example." We forget that we are not by ourselves in all this; Jesus is with us, through the Holy Spirit, helping us. He did not come to earth just to die on the Cross for our sins; He also came to give us an example and pattern for living life on earth according to the Father's original plan, and the power to live it out. When we read biblical accounts of His life with this in mind, we gain a new way of looking at both the Bible and Jesus' earthly life. This new perspective shows us what Jesus did in particular situations—and what we can do in similar ones with His help.

Our question throughout this journey will be, "How do I turn my spiritual routine into a sacred romance?" Christ comes to us throughout the day in many ways. He wants us to meet with Him and experience the love He has for us. As we develop eyes to see Him in the different moments of the day, our spiritual practices take on a new light; they become ways to enfold ourselves in His love and deepen our love for Him. The deeper this love grows, the more we will want to be with Him; and the more we are with Him, the more we become like Him.

Far from any routine this cycle of love, encounter, and change is a wonderful, sacred romance—where each meeting with Christ becomes more and more like a lovers' rendezvous. So let's begin—our Beloved is eagerly waiting for us just around the corner!

"Once God's sweetness has been tasted, it draws us to the pure love of God more than our needs compel us to love him. Thus we begin to say, 'We now love God, not for our necessity, for we ourselves have tasted and know how sweet the Lord is.'"

—Bernard of Clairvaux (1090–1153)[2]

HOW DO I TURN MY SPIRITUAL ROUTINE INTO A SACRED ROMANCE?

rendezvous

Day 1

A LOVE STORY

Jesus replied: "'Love the Lord your God with all your heart and with all your soul and with all your mind.' This is the first and greatest commandment. And the second is like it: 'Love your neighbor as yourself'" (Matt. 22:37-39).

Everybody loves a love story! I'm not talking about grocery store romance novels near the checkout stand with pictures of beautiful women being swept off their feet by heroic men. That's fantasy. I'm talking about a story of genuine love. It might be the story of high school sweethearts who fall in love as teenagers and commit themselves to the marriage of a lifetime. It might be the story of two football players whose lives are torn apart by cancer. It might be the story of a saint who pours every free minute of his or her life into meeting the needs of suffering people.

Love stories differ in an infinite number of ways, but they share common characteristics. Every love story has a subject, an object, and the love that binds them. Life has a way of complicating every love story. Obstacles test or confound love. Great effort must be exerted to overcome those obstacles. Love stories with happy endings usually speak of true love triumphing over every obstacle and binding the main characters even more strongly together.

This book falls clearly in the category of a love story. Christ is the subject and the main character of the story. We are the objects of His interest. Indescribable, unspeakable, unimaginable love brings us together with Him. As in every love story, life has a way of complicating the plot.

Think about the things that complicate your life right now. Maybe your thoughts turn to family responsibilities or issues, trouble at

15

work, stress with the kids, health concerns, problems with the neighbors, unpaid bills, or an out-of-control schedule. That last one describes most people I know! The list of complicating issues in people's lives can be rather long. I don't want you to focus too much on these issues, but I do want you to be aware of them.

These complications in our lives can create roadblocks that impede our awareness of Christ's love for us. They can also hinder our effectiveness in loving Christ the way we want. Many of us are so busy or so overwhelmed with life's problems that all of our energy, attention, time, and effort go to dealing with them.

> "For our soul is so specially loved by [God] that it surpasses the knowledge of all beings—that is to say that there is no being made that can know how much and how sweetly and how tenderly our Maker loves us."
>
> Julian of Norwich (c. 1342–after 1416)[3]

That's where this book can help. It will refocus Christ and His love front and center so we can see Him in new ways. It will provide tools for breaking through those roadblocks in our lives, so we can reconnect with Christ in meaningful ways every day. This book won't take away all of our problems; only heaven can do that! It will, however, help us encounter Christ in new places and experience His love in the midst of our current situations.

This book will help us encounter Christ in new places and experience His love in the midst of our current situations.

I flew home yesterday and landed in the midst of a windstorm. Flags stood at attention. Trees and bushes shook vigorously. Our plane rocked back and forth and up and down to maintain a steady glide path onto the runway. The minute our wheels touched down I noticed the wind had no effect on the airport's tower. It's footing of steel and concrete buried deep in the ground gave it the ability to resist the wind's fury.

Life happens to all of us. So, yes, the winds of life will blow on us. Yes, we will be shaken at times. However, we can have a footing in Christ that will plant us so deeply in Him that we will be able to resist the wind's fury. We'll explore strategies in this book for holding steady through the fiercest windstorms life throws at us.

Look back over your list of complications. See them as wind gusts blowing on you. Now remember that Christ's love for you anchors you as firmly in Him as steel and concrete anchor the airport tower. You're safe in His love!

When I think about a true love story, I always think about the love of my life—Sue. Since we were married, we have spent nearly every day together for more than three decades. I don't look like one of those guys on the cover of the romance novels at the grocery store. I'm sure Sue doesn't feel swept off her feet with indescribable romance on most workdays. But we love one another deeply.

Our love for each other does not still the winds of life. The winds come, and they sometimes can complicate or frustrate our love. But we survive together when those same winds seem to drive so many other lovers apart, because we find ways to connect and reconnect daily. If I'm out of town, we call and e-mail each other. If one of us has a work deadline, we get the job done then make time to be together. We've determined that come what may, we're going to stay together for life. Why? Because we love each other with a love that grows day by day.

Our friends recently celebrated their 40th wedding anniversary. When I asked Bill the secret of their marital success, he responded, "Iced tea." "Iced tea?" I asked. "What does iced tea have to do with a successful marriage?" I'll never forget Bill's response. He said that at the end of nearly every day for the past 40 years, he and Ruth sat in the swing on the back porch with glasses of iced tea, just spending time together. Now that's a line right out of a love story if I ever heard one!

Christ loves you. The Bible is certain about that. And I'll bet you love Him, too, or you wouldn't be reading this book. For the next 40 days we're going to talk about strategies to spice up your love with Christ so you can encounter Him in new ways. These strategies won't assume everything in your life is calm; it probably isn't. But these tools will give you more opportunities to love Christ and experience His love for you amid your daily challenges.

Day 1

Remember: Christ loves you, and you love Him.

Love the Lord your God with all your heart and with all your soul and with all your mind (Matt. 22:37).

Day 2

RESET YOUR LENS

In reply Jesus declared, "I tell you the truth, no one can see the kingdom of God unless he is born again" (John 3:3).

Robert was deeply in love with his wife, Gale. But someone new entered his life. He wasn't expecting it and hadn't planned for it to happen. But this year love hit his heart with a new affection. He had never experienced anything quite like it! Just when he thought his life was complete, he fell head-over-heels in love with a new girl. He thought about her all the time and stopped by her house as often as possible. No, Robert was not having a midlife crisis. He was just finding out that being a grandparent was exactly that—grand!

The minute Robert laid eyes on his granddaughter, Emily, for the first time, he knew he would love her for a lifetime. She was full of life and energy. Robert loved being with her to—well—just be with her. She couldn't perform many baby tricks at first, but that was all right. She was perfect just the way she was.

When Jesus met one night with Nicodemus, He illustrated His spiritual lesson by talking about a baby's birth. Emily came into her family's life just the way every other baby enters this world—she was born. Jesus told Nicodemus that new spiritual life in God looks a lot like being born all over again. That's where we get the term *born again*. When a person accepts Jesus Christ as personal Savior, everything changes. The new birth opens a whole new spiritual world for us to explore and grow in.

If you've been a Christian for very long, you already know that. Simple truth, right? Sure it is. And yet, we don't always live by that truth. Too often we place so much emphasis on the event of being

19

born again that we fail to give proper attention to the growth that follows new birth. Growth always follows birth.

Emily and her mother, Amy, only stayed at the hospital a couple of days following Emily's birth. Then Ryan, the father of the family, took them home, along with the flowers, balloons, and baby gear. Ryan, Amy, and Emily began their family life together, and Emily has grown physically and mentally every day since. That's the way new life happens. A radio ad amused me the other day because its message struck home. In the ad a mother called her married daughter and scolded her for not e-mailing pictures of the new baby. The daughter said, "I just sent you pictures 30 minutes ago." The mother quickly replied, "Yes, I got those. I want *recent* pictures!" Babies grow quickly!

We Christians may be tempted to place too much emphasis on the born-again event because we misunderstand why Jesus came to earth. A famous radio talk show host recently asked his listening audience, "Why did Jesus come to earth?" Most listeners replied, "To die for our sins." That's true. The movie *The Passion of the Christ* brought that truth to life in a powerful new way. However, that's not the whole story.

Focusing only on Jesus' death on the Cross fails to give proper emphasis to His life and ministry. He gave us a wealth of examples through His actions, reactions, attitudes, and responses to life's situations. He gave us a wealth of information through His teaching and preaching ministry. By paying special attention to Jesus' life and ministry we can better learn how to grow in our spiritual walk with Him. For that reason, just as the introduction promised, this book will look closely at the life and ministry of Jesus. Each day's Scripture reading will come from one of the Gospels. So you'll only need Matthew, Mark, Luke, and John for your primary daily reading.

Once we've been born again, our new life in Christ places us in a growing relationship with Him for as long as we live. We grow spiritually just as a newborn grows physically and mentally. That's why I titled this chapter "Reset Your Lens." Like most cameras, mine has a close-up and a wide-angle setting. The first allows me to zero in on my subject. The second gives me a panoramic view of the whole landscape.

Rather than thinking of the Christian life only as having our sins forgiven and being born again (both of which are vitally important), we must reset the lens of our mind to a more panoramic view. This wider view takes in the whole spectrum of life and growth in our Christian journey. The Christian life is exactly that—a journey of exploration that will consume us for a lifetime of experiences and encounters with Christ.

The Christian life is exactly that—a journey of exploration that will consume us for a lifetime of experiences and encounters with Christ.

I said yesterday that this book explores the love story between you and Christ. Today I want to call your attention to the relationship you have with Him daily. Just like any other relationship, it takes place over a lifetime. Your new birth occurred at a certain time; your spiritual life in Him will grow and expand from that time until you join Him in eternity. All you need to do is draw closer to Him and watch the many ways you grow as His love changes you day by day.

Day 2

Remember: Your Christian life began with a new birth and will grow and expand for the rest of your life.

I tell you the truth, no one can see the kingdom of God unless he is born again (John 3:3).

Day 3

DON'T JUST "DO IT"

Jesus, full of the Holy Spirit, returned from the Jordan and was led by the Spirit in the desert, where for forty days he was tempted by the devil. He ate nothing during those days, and at the end of them he was hungry (Luke 4:1-2).

Media ads for sports clothes, sports shoes, and sports drinks all urge us to just get on the field, the court, or the track and perform our best. "Do it," they say. These ads imply that we can excel at the sport of our choice if we add equal doses of effort, willpower, and determination. Pep talks are what produce Olympic dreams and state championships. We want to believe the ads. However, no sports outfit, shoe, or fancy bottled drink can give the skill we need to excel at our favorite sport. There's more to it than that.

That same line of "do it" reasoning found its way into the Christian community. I used to think this was due to Christian preachers and thinkers watching too many episodes of *Superman* or *The Lone Ranger*. Now I know that this reasoning found its way into our religious pep talks long before either hero ever hit the television airwaves.

This terrible error actually crept into our Christian thinking about 500 years ago during the Protestant Reformation. About that time we began to focus more on our individual faith and less on the Christian community. What's more, we sometimes emphasized human effort over the Holy Spirit's empowerment and direction. Like the message of the media ads, Christians came to believe they needed to add equal doses of effort, willpower, and determination to their spiritual activity. This would assure the spiritual results they desired.

Now don't get me wrong; the Reformation and, later, the Enlightenment did bring Christianity many new insights. Most furthered the cause of Christ and resulted in a more biblical faith. But the importance placed on individual faith and human effort may have resulted in the biggest mistake we made—an almost exclusive emphasis on a *personal* belief in Jesus Christ.

Wow! You didn't expect me to say that, did you? Isn't personal faith in Jesus Christ a good thing? Yes, it is—that is, until we limit Christian living to being just "Jesus and me." When that happens, we tend to make the faith journey from here to heaven a solitary one—just Jesus and me and no one else. We may give some credit to Jesus, but really we are little more than self-contained followers who succeed by sheer grit and determination. We'll make it to the end without help from anyone—"No, thank you—I can do it by myself."

Jesus never lived or taught a religion of rugged individualism. He does not intend for us to make the faith journey all by ourselves or solely on willpower. In our Scripture for today we read of Jesus' temptations. Notice that He did not face this challenge alone. The Holy Spirit accompanied Him when He went into the desert and when He resisted the devil's advances. Later in Matthew, we read that the Father sent angels to minister to Him (4:11). Jesus received help before, during, and after His ordeal.

> "This is true perfection: not to avoid a wicked life because . . . we servilely fear punishment, nor to do good because we hope for rewards. . . . [but] we regard falling from God's friendship as the only thing dreadful and we consider becoming God's friend the only thing worthy of honor and desire."
> —Gregory of Nyssa (c. 335-c. 395)[4]

Christ never expects us to live our Christian lives under our own power. We have the Holy Spirit just as Jesus did. The Spirit lives in our hearts, empowers our efforts, and directs our steps. What's more, we have other Christian brothers and sisters to walk with us and assist us through the trials of life. While it is certainly true that faith in Jesus Christ requires a personal commitment, we can never succeed as Christians by ourselves. We need the Spirit, and we need each other. Help from others may come from one Christian friend or family member, from a small group of Christians, or from an entire community of faith. We will explore each of these possibilities in the weeks ahead.

Today's devotional thought delivers a key principle for this book. That's why I placed it at the very beginning. You see, next week we're going to start talking about Christian practices and activities that flow from our love for God. The danger always lurks in the shadows for us to think that our performance of these practices or activities somehow earns us favor with God. If we're not careful, we can fall into the trap of trying to earn our salvation by properly performing certain rituals. Jesus condemned this practice among the Pharisees (see Matt. 15:1-9). They followed all of their religious rules and traditions with diligence but totally neglected their love relationship with God. Jesus has no more favor with a performance-based religion today than when He walked the dusty paths of this world.

So don't just "do it." Acknowledge your human limitations. Admit your weakness. Accept that you need the constant direction and empowerment of the Spirit of Christ along with the helping hand of other believers.

Day 3

Remember: You can't do it alone; you need the help of the Spirit and of other Christian believers.

Jesus, full of the Holy Spirit, returned from the Jordan and was led by the Spirit (Luke 4:1).

Day 4

HOW GREEN IS YOUR THUMB?

While a large crowd was gathering and people were coming to Jesus from town after town, he told this parable: "A farmer went out to sow his seed. As he was scattering the seed, some fell along the path; it was trampled on, and the birds of the air ate it up. Some fell on rock, and when it came up, the plants withered because they had no moisture. Other seed fell among thorns, which grew up with it and choked the plants. Still other seed fell on good soil. It came up and yielded a crop, a hundred times more than was sown." When he said this, he called out, "He who has ears to hear, let him hear" (Luke 8:4-8).

Growing up on a farm gave me many experiences in our family vegetable garden. We grew just about every vegetable that would take root in our region of the country. Carrots, green beans, lima beans, peas, squash, okra, corn, potatoes, and pumpkin topped the list. We even grew fruit, like tomatoes. That's right. Tomatoes are a fruit, not a vegetable. We ate, froze, or canned most of what we raised and gave the rest to family, friends, and transient farm workers.

Growing a garden requires only a few basic steps. First, you prepare the ground. This includes breaking up the soil and trenching it into rows. Next, you plant the seed. You must space them the proper distance from one another, depending on the seed type. You also must bury them to the proper depth. Third, you often need to build a fence around the garden to keep hungry animals out. Fourth, you pull the weeds that spring up around the tender plants. Further, you need to water the garden if rains do not water it enough. Finally, you pick the produce when it is ripe.

Our culture says people who are good at gardening flowers, fruit, or vegetables have a green thumb. Gardeners do not actually have thumbs colored green, but they do have a special skill at making things grow. In the past we said growth always follows new life. Today we want to highlight our responsibility to nurture the spiritual life Christ gives us with our gift of new birth.

*We have a responsibility to nurture the spiritual life
Christ gives us with our gift of new birth.*

The Scripture reading for today features one of Jesus' parables. He told of a farmer who planted seed much like my family planted in our garden. Jesus called attention to the four locations where the seed landed. Some seed fell on the path, some on rocks, some among thorns, and some on good soil. Only the good soil produced a bountiful harvest.

Jesus then, in verses 11-15, related the meaning of the parable. The seed represented the word of God. The types of soil represented various human hearts and their responses to God's message. Everyone heard the message but responded in different ways. Only the last group made the most of their opportunity.

In the days ahead, this book will offer several ways to prepare our heart and life so we can make the most of our opportunity to be in a close personal relationship with Christ. He offers us the gift of knowing Him; we just have to accept that gift and faithfully act on it. In His parable Jesus warned of the intrusions of the devil, times of testing, life's worries, riches, and pleasures. All of these intruders pose as great a danger today as they did in Jesus' day. We must put our lives in order so we can avoid the crop-killing effects these intruders bring.

I began today's reading talking about gardening, not to give a lesson in horticulture, but to make connections between growing a garden and growing a Christian. They share several things in common:

- Just as a gardener prepares the ground, we must prepare our heart to receive Christ's messages to us. Christ sends us special love notes each day. We must expect them and look for them. The more we do this, the better we will be able to see them.

- Just as a gardener plants seed, we must receive Christ's messages and plant them in our heart and mind. That means we must hear Christ's words to us, make them a part of our life, and act on them.

- Just as a gardener builds a fence to protect the garden from outside intruders, we must set up barriers that keep the devil, times of testing, life's worries, riches, and pleasures from controlling what we think and do. These intruders will come, no question about that. But we do not need to let them throw us off balance spiritually.

- Just as a gardener pulls weeds that spring up from the soil, we must tend to our heart and life daily to guard against intruders creeping up from within and hindering our spiritual growth and effectiveness. Bad attitudes, resentfulness, oversensitive feelings, and ill will toward others hinder spiritual growth. Remember, fences guard against intruders from without; weeding takes care of problems that spring from within.

- Just as a gardener waters the garden, we must nurture our spiritual life from the many options Christ offers us. Bible reading, prayer, meditation, worship, the sacraments, and Christian fellowship all nurture spiritual life. We will explore these and many others over the next six weeks.

- Just as a bountiful harvest rewards a gardener's efforts, our life will also produce a spiritual harvest to the glory of God.

We will discuss more about each of these observations in the days ahead. Today we need to set our heart and mind on following the example of a good gardener. We must treat our life as a garden where we can grow spiritual fruit for God and His good purposes.

So often my friends comment when a houseplant dies, "Oh well, I guess I don't have a green thumb." They assume good gardeners come into this world with preloaded gardening skills. Not so. Good gardeners develop their skills. We, too, must nurture our skills at growing our relationship with Christ.

Pray today that Christ will give you a vision of His desire to help you grow in your walk with Him. Once you have that vision clearly focused in your mind, pray that He will help you be receptive to all of the many ways He wants to assist you in your growth.

Day 4

Remember: Gardening is a learned skill.

A farmer went out to sow his seed (Luke 8:5).

Day 5

THE MATRIX

When Jesus heard what had happened, he withdrew by boat privately to a solitary place. Hearing of this, the crowds followed him on foot from the towns. When Jesus landed and saw a large crowd, he had compassion on them (Matt. 14:13-14).

I recently sat at a gate in Chicago O'Hare International Airport and watched the people sitting around me. A man to my left sat quietly by himself and read a book. Another man sat across the aisle from me and searched the Internet on his computer. Three ladies sat to my right and engaged in lively conversation. A man to my far right checked with his office on his cell phone. A young lady in front of me listened to her favorite songs on her iPod. Some people just sat idly and watched travelers go by. As you can tell, I simply took it all in.

There we were—all of us waiting for the same airplane to take us to the same location. But at that moment we all had different levels of engagement with our surroundings, with technology, and with each other. Some seized the moment for social interaction, business, solitude, education, entertainment, or relaxation. Others put their minds in neutral and zoned out.

Our lives are much like that during an average day, aren't they? We can go through our daily activities with our minds in neutral, simply zoned out and going through the motions. Or we can fully engage in what we are doing and seize each moment to accomplish something worthwhile. The choice is up to us.

Unfortunately, too many people become such creatures of habit that they remain accomplished fugitives from themselves. They get so numb to their daily routines that they check items off their to-do lists without thinking about what's really taking place. That happens to me too. Sometimes I'll be staring into space as if in deep thought, and my wife will draw me back to reality with the all-important question wives often ask: "What are you thinking about?" I stop and think about what I was thinking. "Nothing," I finally say. I had spent the last five minutes thinking about absolutely nothing. There's nothing wrong with that once in a while. But it can be a real problem if we throw our brains into neutral for long periods of time to avoid fully engaging life. I'm afraid too many people get so busy being busy that they do not spend enough time productively interacting with the people and events in their daily lives.

Unfortunately too many people become such creatures of habit that they become accomplished fugitives from themselves.

Now I'm sure you're as busy as I am. On some days my schedule looks like the flight plan of an international airliner. I couldn't add one more meeting or event to the day if I had to. I never just sit and wonder what to do with my time. I imagine you don't either!

Sometimes I'm alone. Usually I'm with my wife, a best friend, a group of Christian believers, or people from my community. These people form the matrix in which I live. This matrix is a web connecting me with individuals and with groups at work, at church, and in my town.

Living our faith in Christ, as well as growing in that faith, is not just one more activity to add to all the others we do each day. It's something we do *amid* our daily activities. It's fully engaging in our matrix of relationships and interactions. It's deciding to take part in our matrix rather than get lost in the monotony of daily routine.

Our Bible reading for today illustrates this truth in Jesus' life. He'd just received terrible news: His cousin John the Baptist had been murdered. Jesus needed time alone to regroup. In an attempt to draw away, He found himself being pursued by thousands of followers. He had every right to flee to the wilderness and withdraw from all human contact. But He chose not to do that. Instead He fully engaged in the moment, taught the people, presented deeper truth to His disciples, and performed one of the greatest miracles of His ministry.

Everyone remembers the wonder of the feeding of the 5,000 men plus their families as recorded in Matt. 14:13-21, Mark 6:32-44, Luke 9:10-17, and John 6:1-13. Few of us place it in the setting of a day when Jesus desperately needed to get away and be alone, when the crowds continued to invade His personal space, and when the disciples continued to misunderstand what His ministry was all about.

In the midst of a hurried schedule, bad news, and a family tragedy, Jesus seized the moment and used it to create a spiritual encounter with His Father. This led to spiritual growth in the lives of His disciples and followers. The principle here is simply this—we've got to keep our eyes peeled through the ordinariness of every day for an encounter with Christ. As we live in the matrix of our relationships, we must continually ask, "How can I encounter Christ here?"

Think of it like this. Our lives flow back and forth between various types of relationships throughout the day. Sometimes we're alone. At other times we're with a trusted friend, in a small group of Christian friends, with the entire faith community at church, or at work or play in the world. We can encounter Christ, learn from Him, and grow in Him at every one of these interactions in many different ways. Like darts on a dartboard, our schedule tosses us into a variety of settings with people every day. We flow back and forth between these settings all day long.

Over the next five weeks, we will explore spiritual growth and development in these social settings. The goal of the book is to teach how to encounter Christ in each of these different settings. These encounters or rendezvous will span an entire lifetime and will result in our becoming more Christlike.

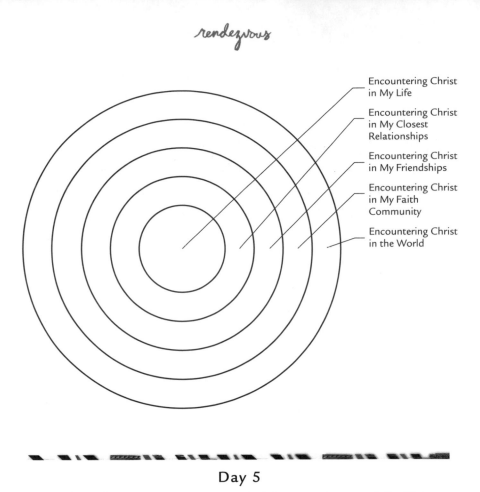

Encountering Christ in My Life

Encountering Christ in My Closest Relationships

Encountering Christ in My Friendships

Encountering Christ in My Faith Community

Encountering Christ in the World

Day 5

Remember: Keep your eyes peeled for Jesus in your daily life!

*When Jesus landed and saw a large crowd,
he had compassion on them* (Matt. 14:14).

"In quiet and silence the faithful soul makes progress,

the hidden meanings of the Scriptures become clear,

and the eyes weep with devotion every night.

Even as one learns to grow still, he draws closer to the

Creator and farther from the hurly-burly of the world.

As one divests himself of friends and acquaintances,

he is visited by God and his holy angels."

—Thomas à Kempis (c. 1380–1471)[5]

ENCOUNTERING CHRIST IN
MY LIFE

rendezvous

Day 6

QUIET CONVERSATIONS

After he had dismissed them, he went up on a mountainside by himself to pray. When evening came, he was there alone (Matt. 14:23).

I had a fantasy as a child of being stranded on a desert island. I guess it all started when I saw the movie *Robinson Crusoe*. It seemed so simple—I could just do what I wanted to do without all of the obligations of civilization. I could explore the island all day and watch the stars at night. I could eat indigenous fruit and grow vegetables in a garden (see Day 4 for details on how I'd do that!). Robinson Crusoe seemed to get along pretty well; I figured I could do the same. I never considered the possibility of snakes, boars, and hurricanes. More recently, Tom Hanks in the movie *Castaway* woke me from my island fantasy. He got really bored and ran out of things to do on his island!

Now I've pretty much given up on the idea of moving to a desert island. I'd want my wife with me if I ever decided to relocate. Maybe I could settle for just a few weeks away from cell phones, e-mails, fax messages, schedules, school functions, church functions, and yardwork! I'll bet you can identify with me.

This week we are going to explore ways we encounter Christ in our private world. The word *quiet* appears in every title of this week's readings because Jesus said our time with God should be a private matter (Matt. 6:6). In this private world it's just God and us communicating and interacting. We cannot stay there however, because God didn't create us to live our entire lives in solitary confinement. The total solitude in *Castaway* drove Tom Hanks to conversing with a volleyball, and prisoners lose touch with reality when left in solitary confinement for very long. But small doses of solitude prove essential to good mental and spiritual health.

People feel differently about being alone. Some see it as a negative thing and feel lonely. Others see it as a positive thing and enjoy the solitude. It depends on how you look at it. When you think about what you don't have—companionship—that's loneliness. When you think about what you have—quietness—that's solitude.

> "Prayer is the superabundance of the heart. It is brim-full and running over with love and praise, as once it was with Mary, when the Word took root in her body. So too, our heart breaks out into a Magnificat."
> —André Louf (1929-)[6]

Jesus lived a busy life and conducted an active daily ministry. When we read the biblical accounts of Jesus' ministry, we see Him surrounded by people and their needs most of the time. But no one, not even Jesus, can live like that all of the time. We must have time alone with God.

In our Scripture reading for today, we see Jesus getting away from ministry, crowds of people, and even His disciples to enjoy solitude. Jesus needed to be alone and enjoy a quiet conversation with His Father. He could only take so many ministry opportunities, so many needs, and so many people for so long. Then He had to withdraw from everything and regroup with His Father in prayer.

Jesus' prayer life must have been contagious, because His disciples wanted to learn how to pray as He did (Luke 11:1). He called prayer personal communication with the Father. It varies, as does our communication with other people.

- Sometimes we pray to praise God for who He is. At other times we wish to thank Him for what He has done or is doing in our world or our lives.

- Sometimes we bring God the needs of friends or loved ones. At other times we come with our own needs.
- Sometimes we have an inner desire for fellowship with our Creator and Friend. At other times an emergency or difficult situation drives us to prayer.
- Sometimes we pray for adequate strength for the task at hand. At other times a sense of our own inability to do anything right completely overwhelms us.
- Sometimes we pray with well-formed sentences and carefully selected words. At other times groans and cries for help fill our prayers.

Jesus taught us almost everything we know about prayer. He modeled many prayer principles for His followers. He directed us to pray as naturally as we breathe (18:1). He said we pray to fellowship with God, not to impress others with our ability to articulate words (Matt. 6:7).

The elements for a successful prayer life appear in the Lord's Prayer found in Matthew. Just before the prayer Jesus teaches that quiet conversations with God are a private matter, not a public performance (vv. 5-6). Then from the prayer we discover several things: We must approach God as our Heavenly Father (v. 9). We must reverence and honor Him (v. 9). We pledge ourselves to live as citizens of God's kingdom while on this earth and follow His will as carefully as the angels in heaven follow it (v. 10). We recognize our dependence upon Him for life's provisions (v. 11). We need His forgiveness of our sins and shortcomings and must manifest this same forgiving attitude toward those who fail us (v. 12). God will be disposed toward forgiving and helping us in the same way we are disposed toward those who do us wrong (v. 14). We recognize the power and pull of temptation and seek His help in resisting it (v. 13). Finally, we need God's help in maintaining victory over Satan and all the forces of evil (v. 13).

During His earthly ministry, Jesus often talked with His Father. He drew away from the crowds or spent the early morning hours in prayer (Luke 6:12). He waited before the Father prior to every big decision, such as the selection of His disciples (v. 13). No matter how busy His schedule kept Him, He did not allow it to crowd out His time with the Father (Mark 6:46). He prayed conversationally, the way He talked with His friends (John 17:1-26). He unburdened His heart, then asked the Father to answer as He saw best (Luke 22:42).

The Bible gives us no preferable posture for praying. We can sit, stand, walk, or kneel—whatever manner is most comfortable for us to communicate with God. The Bible does not prescribe a particular time of day for prayer. If we prefer the morning, we can set aside time then. If we think best in the evening, we can talk with God at the end of the day. We can also pray during breaks in our daily workflow or while driving, flying, or waiting at the doctor's office. A morning or evening walk is also a good opportunity for prayer. Our lives can brim with prayer, praying whenever we get the chance at any time night or day.

No matter why we come to God or which words we use once we get there, He welcomes us with open arms and says, "Come now, let us reason together" (Isa. 1:18). He loves for us to come to Him, and He delights in talking with us while we are together. Jesus taught us to come often and stay as long as we can. I talk to my wife daily, not because I have to, but because I love her and I want to. The same is true as we meet with Christ just to talk. It's love that draws us together—Christ's love for us and our love for Him.

So find time to talk to Christ daily. As you do, the love you share with Him will grow and you will start to see Him in many new and wonderful ways.

Day 6

Remember: Jesus needed quiet conversations with His Father and so do we.

He went up on a mountainside by himself to pray (Matt. 14:23).

Day 7

QUIET LISTENING

One of those days Jesus went out to a mountainside to pray,
and spent the night praying to God (Luke 6:12).

I'm sitting near a lake right now quietly listening. At least 20 different types of birds sing in the trees above. Several bugs pierce the air with a buzz of activity. A woodpecker works away on a new hole. Crickets, frogs, geese, and squirrels play around the lakeshore. Fish slap the water as they break the surface. The wind rustles through the tree leaves. A farmer hammers nails on a shed across the lake.

My ears are so conditioned to hear street clatter, music, voices, and other sounds of the civilized world that they tend to tune out the world of nature. But if I stop and begin to quietly listen, this other world of sounds suddenly springs to life for me.

Yesterday we discussed prayer. We considered what it means to talk to Christ. But prayer also involves listening—quietly listening for Christ to talk to us. Quietly listening involves more than just leaving a few seconds of silence at the end of our side of the conversation. It means breaking our addiction to noise by leaving the radio, television, CD player, iPod, cell phone, and computer off. It means tuning those sounds out and tuning in the sound of Christ's voice.

> *Prayer also involves listening—*
> *quietly listening for Christ to talk to us.*

Hearing Christ's voice remains one of the greatest privileges of life. Followers of other world religions pray to their god(s), but Christians and Jews pray differently. Prayer in most religions of the world

41

remains a one-way street—followers talk but do not receive direct answers. They usually pray to appease a god's anger or to win favor. Christians and Jews see prayer as a two-way street, with God both hearing and answering, like talking on the telephone. It becomes a time of intimate friendship.

Once we have said what we want to say to Christ, we must learn to sit quietly and listen for His response to us. A nine-year-old boy asked me recently how he could recognize Christ's voice. This important question comes with a simple answer. You learn to recognize His voice by spending time with Him and discovering what makes His voice unique. I am amazed at how quickly babies learn to recognize their mom's and dad's voices in a room full of people. Babies make that association on their own. They learn their parents' voices through a daily close relationship with them.

Prayer offers us an opportunity to share our needs and concerns with Christ. Once we stop talking and quietly listen for His reply, we realize that

- Christ can help us better understand our situation. Our problem may seem large and vague before we pray about it. Christ focuses the picture for us, like adjusting the image on a computer screen.
- Christ can help us put our situation in perspective. Our problem may seem unsolvable before we pray about it. Christ lets the air out of an inflated problem, like letting the air out of a balloon. He brings it down to a manageable size.
- Christ reminds us that we are not facing our situation alone. He tells us He is with us and helping us. He comes to stand beside us, like a friend coming to our aid.
- Christ gives us the right attitude or frame of mind from which to see things. We often come to Christ looking at things in a self-centered way. Time with Him turns us around so we can see things the way He does.

- Quietly listening gives Christ the chance to work in our life or in circumstances in ways that He would not do if we did not come to Him and wait before Him. The all-powerful Creator of the universe chooses to work through us as we open up to His will and purpose. Prayer opens channels for Christ to act as we listen to His voice.

We can do several things to make quiet listening a part of our lives. Instead of concluding our prayer time with a moment of silence, we can extend the session and listen quietly for His gentle voice. Pausing and listening every now and then throughout prayer is another option. This may actually work better than doing all of the talking first. Christ will honor our efforts and speak with us as we listen.

Silence and contemplation carry more value than simply logging time.

The amount of time we set aside for quiet listening will depend on our individual needs or circumstances. Silence and contemplation carry more value than simply logging time. Here are some other ideas for quiet listening:

- Leaving the television, radio, CD player, iPod, and other media off at certain times to clear our minds of noise.
- Visiting a park or nature center to commune with Christ away from the busy life of the city
- Driving to work or just out in the country in silence while listening for Christ's voice
- Taking a retreat from a busy schedule, other people, and obligations
- Turning off all activity and noise on Sunday except going to worship

We can expect to experience some signs of media or noise withdrawal as we practice quiet listening. Our son, Brent, completed a school assignment in the ninth grade that required him to avoid watching television for two weeks. I was not sure he, or his parents, would survive! Since that assignment I have guarded my schedule carefully and always found time for the important practice of quiet listening.

Remember our friends I told you about on Day 1 who drank countless glasses of iced tea on the back porch swing? They did not spend 40 years together over glasses of iced tea talking all of the time. Sometimes they just sat and enjoyed being in each other's company. Neither spoke words, but both enjoyed the fellowship of simply being together in one another's presence. Think about that the next time you meet with Christ. Enjoy just being together!

Day 7

Remember: Christ speaks to us; we must tune our ears to hear Him.

One of those days Jesus went out to a mountainside to pray,
and spent the night praying to God (Luke 6:12).

Day 8

QUIET READING

He went to Nazareth, where he had been brought up, and on the Sabbath day he went into the synagogue, as was his custom. And he stood up to read (Luke 4:16).

I travel frequently with my job. Anytime I'm away from home, especially if I'm out of the country, I find ways to connect with my wife, Sue. These days we connect through e-mail. Everywhere I go I can find a café with a computer or an Internet shop where I quickly log on and read my latest e-mail from my wife. Before e-mail, we'd communicate with each other through fax machines. In many foreign countries the phone lines over which faxes travel were not reliable. I sometimes had to wait for as many as 20 attempts before a readable copy came through, but the frustration paid off when I got that fax from Sue in hand.

What do you suppose I do when I get a fax or an e-mail from Sue? Lay it aside for a later read? No. I read it immediately. Then I read it again and again throughout the day, pausing and thinking about every word. Why so much attention to this single piece of paper? Because it contains a message written just to me from the most important person in my world. Loving relationships thrive on communication.

The same principle applies to our relationship with God. God is a God of words. He spoke our world into existence. He talked with Adam and Eve during their evening walks through the garden. He communicated throughout the Bible with those who reverenced Him. He does not leave us guessing about who He is, what He is like, or how best to relate to Him. He makes all of this plain and simple for the smallest child to understand. Why? Because He uses words—words we can understand.

We are a privileged generation. We have a copy of God's words in a book. This book tells us of the reality and wonder of God. It tells us everything we need to know for a close personal relationship with Him.

Unfortunately this book gets lost with all of the other books on the shelf at home. And time with this book gets lost with all of the other things we have to do in a day. So our e-mail from God often goes unread.

Our Scripture reading for today finds Jesus in His hometown of Nazareth at the opening of His ministry. He went to the synagogue on the designated day of worship just as He always did. The synagogue priest asked Him to read the Scripture lesson for the day. He rolled the scroll to Isa. 61:1-2 and read it. You can read the rest of the account in Luke 4. I want us to think about verses 16-17. How is it that Jesus could find such an appropriate Scripture reading at a moment's notice? Because He read it frequently, knew its message well, and knew where to find specific passages of Scripture for specific needs.

> "Read very slowly. You do not move from one passage to another, not until you have *sensed* the very heart of what you have read. You may then want to take that portion of Scripture . . . and turn it into prayer."
>
> Madame Guyon (1648—1717)[7]

As we read the Gospel accounts, we realize that Jesus used Scripture often in His ministry. Earlier in Luke 4 we see Him meeting the devil head on during His concentrated period of temptation. His primary weapon against the devil? Scripture. Jesus often answered His critics with Scripture. He comforted His disciples and others with passages from the Bible. He even quoted Ps. 22 as He hung on the Cross. No question about it. Jesus read the Bible often, committed passages to memory, and had a command of its message to apply to people's needs at just the right time.

Jesus came to earth for many reasons. One of them was to give us an example to live by. Jesus' habit of reading the Bible offers us a pattern for our own lives. He didn't read the Bible out of obligation or ritual. He read it to connect with His Father and hear His words of love, support, and reassurance again and again. He cherished those words as nourishment for spiritual life.

Jesus' habit of reading the Bible offers us a pattern for our own lives.

Today's devotional reading is not meant to make us feel guilty. We can get that feeling easily enough from all the demands placed on us by work, society, and the pressures of life. Bible reading is not just another item to check off our to-do list. God provides the Bible as His love letter to us. It's just like the faxes and e-mails I get from Sue while traveling. I'll walk or ride a bicycle as far as I need to go to get my hands on those communications from the love of my life. The obstacles I overcome on my way to those faxes or e-mails are only minor inconveniences. I remember riding a subway and then a bus across the entire city of Moscow just to get my hands on one fax!

I deal with college students daily. I think I've heard just about every excuse for why an assignment isn't in my hand. When I look at their schedules, I see them functioning fully in society. They go to class, work out in the gym, play sports, eat in the cafeteria, and work at a part- or full-time job. They pretty much do what they want to do in a day. Usually they did not complete their assignment because it did not top their priority list.

We all live busy lives. We all have more obligations in a day than we can humanly meet. So we prioritize and make sure we do the things that require immediate attention. Reading the Bible should be a regular priority. It's not like taking cough medicine, which tastes really bad but is good for you. God's Word connects us with our best Friend in life. It guides us daily and equips us for the temptations and stresses of life. It shows us how to live successfully and pleasing in God's sight. And it comes to our aid in times of need.

Jesus knew the Bible and its message well enough to apply it to every situation He faced. We can do the same. It's never too late to start. The devil lies when he tells us we do not have time, or the Bible is too hard to understand, or we are not qualified to interpret it.

So let's sit down with our love letter from God and read a passage. Then let's quietly listen—as we discussed yesterday—to the voice of the Spirit of Christ as He teaches us. We can next apply what we learn from God's Word to our lives and watch them come back into focus. It is amazing to see how the Spirit takes God's Word and uses it in our lives in such a direct way.

Most people read the Bible during their quiet conversations with God. That usually works well because time is already set aside with our heart and mind tuned to hear God's voice. But we can also hear God's Word

- Reading at the doctor's office or at the airport
- From note cards copied and placed on a mirror, car sun visor, or workstation
- Listening to the Bible on CD while driving
- Singing choruses with biblical texts

Find the methods that work best for you. Whatever you do, remember you've got mail from God! Find time to read it. You will get to know Christ and His love better than ever as you do.

Day 8

Remember: God sends you His love in a letter. Read it.

And he stood up to read (Luke 4:16).

Day 9

QUIET THINKING

After three days they found him in the temple courts, sitting among the teachers, listening to them and asking them questions. Everyone who heard him was amazed at his understanding and his answers (Luke 2:46-47).

Our friend Melanie possesses a special ability to organize things. Never mind what needs organizing. She can look at a situation, examine what needs to be organized, and sort things into logical categories. In no time she has a place for everything and everything in its place. She even labels things in her house so they find their way back to where they belong. Melanie matches the skill of any of those reality television stars who organize messy homes for a living.

When I think of today's topic, I think of Melanie's organizing skills because they're so closely related. You see, Melanie first develops categories, then she places objects in those categories. The same principles apply to quiet thinking. Today's topic gives us an opportunity to examine another aspect of meeting with Christ alone. So far, we've explored our conversations with God, His replies to us, and reading His Word. We've laid our problems, issues, and needs before Him. We've listened to His observations on those matters. And we've read His Word and allowed the Holy Spirit to apply it to our lives.

The next step in meeting with Christ invites us to stop and think reflectively as we sort all of this out and place it into categories for future reference. We must do this not only to preserve what God has said to us but also to experience growth and development in our Christian lives.

In our Scripture lesson for today, Jesus illustrates a benefit of quiet thinking. At the age of 12 He had already spent so much time quietly thinking about the truths of the Bible and the messages He received from His Father in prayer that He amazed the teachers at the Temple with His depth of insight and understanding. In other words, as a young teenager Jesus realized the value of thinking reflectively about spiritual truths, making them a part of His mental processes, and applying them to life.

As a young teenager Jesus realized the value of thinking reflectively about spiritual truths, making them a part of His mental processes, and applying them to life.

I'm always intrigued by verses in the Bible like Luke 5:16, "But Jesus often withdrew to lonely places and prayed." Notice that He unplugged from people and activity often to fellowship with His Father. I believe He used these times not only to pray and listen to His Father's responses but also to sort things out in His head before going back into the flow of society and His public ministry. Jesus continually amazed the crowds with His quick quotations from Scripture for every situation (see Mark 11:18). He could do that because He didn't just read Scripture. He thought about its message and filed its truth for future reference.

Our society does not have a high regard for quiet thinking. We have too many places to go, too many people to see, and too many things to do to stop and quietly reflect on the inner life of the mind and heart. Besides that, serious thinking is for intellectuals, we're told. Contemporary society places much more emphasis on doing than being. So we receive performance awards at school, work, and even church for excelling at an infinite number of tasks. That's the doing side of life. But what about the being side? What about the health and wellbeing of the mind? What about a well-organized and centered inner life?

When I speak of a centered inner life, I'm not referring to yoga or any other eastern religious practices. I'm talking about the Christian method of taking the insights we receive from the Spirit as well as other sources and organizing them in a way that leads to spiritual growth. Christ will meet us in this as well.

Our society does not have a high regard for quiet thinking.

During Jesus' ministry, one of the teachers of the Law asked Him to identify the most important commandment. He answered by calling us to love God and love our neighbor as ourselves (Mark 12:28-30). One of the ways Jesus said we love God is "with all your mind" (v. 30). He no doubt implied many things with this simple phrase. A key activity of the mind involves thinking about what we see, hear, smell, taste, read, and experience every day. Much of the time we allow these sensations and experiences to pass through our consciousness without capturing them into organized thoughts and placing them in cubbyholes for future reference. When we take the time to capture, organize, and file them away, we make them our own for later use.

I am always saddened when I hear Christians say, "I'm just too busy to think." Unfortunately, these people will miss out on the great insights Christ has for them because they choose not to take the time to love Him with their minds. They run from day to day occupying themselves with a myriad of activities, probably having some of the same spiritual experiences repeated due to their lack of attention. They resemble people caught in the Twilight Zone living the same day over and over again.

These people are much like the poor birds living in our backyard. Every spring one of them does the same sad thing. She sees a great spot through our living room window to build her nest. So she flies toward the spot and hits the window. After falling to the ground, she picks herself up, shakes the numbness out of her head, flies back to her original tree branch, and repeats the same thing all over again. Unfortunately, she continues to do this day after day until she kills herself. All the while my wife and I ask each other, "Why doesn't she ever learn?"

I know too many Christians who seem stagnant in their Christian walk. Their commitment to Christ remains unquestioned. Their problem? An overloaded schedule keeps them so busy that they never take the time to just stop and think about what they hear in the Bible, in prayer, in the sermon, in a Christian song or book, or from the Spirit. Life happens too quickly for adequate reflection. Consequently, they languish in their spirit.

Quiet thinking involves sitting alone in a quiet place periodically and sorting through the spiritual insights coming our way, then filing them in cubbyholes of the mind for later access. Try it! You'll be amazed at the connections you'll begin to make between what you're learning today and what you learned a month or a year ago. After a while you'll begin to see a more complete picture of your spiritual life and Christ's involvement in it.

Day 9

Remember: Take time to stop and just think.

Everyone who heard him was amazed at his understanding and his answers (Luke 2:47).

Day 10

QUIET WRITING

And Mary said: "My soul glorifies the Lord and my spirit
rejoices in God my Savior" (Luke 1:46-47).

Sue took up a new habit the week before our granddaughter Mia came into our lives. She sat down with a leather-bound book of blank pages and began writing notes to Mia about important moments shared with her. She plans to give it to her someday as a keepsake. Some of the entries will make Mia laugh, like the time we fed her sweet potatoes and got more on her and us than in her mouth. Some will remind her of her spiritual heritage, like the day I dedicated her back to Jesus. Sue says documenting these special moments is important, and with that I wholeheartedly agree.

We're looking this week at spending special time alone with Christ. We've looked at several different ways we do that. Today we want to talk about quietly writing down our spiritual insights and thoughts. Most books refer to this as journaling, but don't let the term scare you. We're not exploring an exercise in the language arts. We're talking about putting down on paper whatever we want to record about our spiritual journey. We can include random or organized thoughts, daily or spiritual events, spiritual insights, questions, prayer requests, answers to prayer, special Bible verses, Bible questions, challenges from God and our responses to them, hopes, fears, and longings. We can write them by hand in a notebook, loose-leaf binder, or leather-bound journal book. Or we can type them on a computer or typewriter. Some people even record their spiritual insights on a voice recorder. It doesn't matter how we do it or how often. We can do it every day, once a week, or during special spiritual times in our lives. What we must not do is fall into the

53

trap of feeling we have failed if we do not write down our thoughts every day. Getting our spiritual thoughts recorded for later reference is the main thing.

In our Scripture reading for today, Mary the mother of Jesus recorded her thoughts and feelings when she realized God had selected her to bring our Savior to this world. You should read the entire passage in Luke 1:46-55. In her journal entry she worshiped God, recounted some of His actions in human history, and acknowledged the things God values.

Excellent books abound on the subject of Christian journaling, so I will not attempt a thorough coverage of it here. I do, however, want to call attention to the importance of recording our thoughts and connect this exercise to the spiritual practices we discussed earlier.

Quiet writing gives us a tool for reflecting on our time alone with Christ. It becomes a written account of God's working in our life. Perhaps one of the best biblical examples of journaling comes from the Book of Psalms. Here King David and others recorded their spiritual journeys so readers could travel with them through the highs and lows of their lives. The psalms remind us of the seasons of life. David pulled no punches; he told us just how he felt. Some days he praised God to the highest heavens. On other days he questioned God's involvement in his life. The psalms remain popular reading for believers today because of their candor and honesty about the victory and defeat of spiritual life.

> *Quiet writing gives us a tool for reflecting*
> *on our time alone with Christ.*

Quiet writing serves many purposes. Simply putting our thoughts on a computer screen or paper helps us verbalize our feelings so we can understand ourselves and our situations better. Understanding ourselves is often 90 percent of the battle. The Spirit of Christ often uses these moments of self-awareness to reveal new truths about ourselves, our motives, our goals, and the direction our lives are currently heading. He might even throw in some course corrections if we're open to them.

Putting down our thoughts becomes a tangible way to record new insights and discoveries from our times of quiet conversations, quiet listening, quiet reading, and quiet thinking. Writing down our thoughts helps clarify Christ's messages to us. If we fail to make note of them, they will be lost like the seed Jesus referred to in the parable of the sower (Luke 8:4-8).

Writing down our thoughts helps clarify Christ's messages to us.

As with quiet conversations and quiet listening, quiet writing has a way of cutting our problems down to manageable size. The worry zone of our brain has a way of blowing our problems as big as a parade balloon. Writing down the Lord's observations about those problems helps us realize that when He steps between our problems and ourselves, they're not nearly as big as they first appeared.

Looking back over our journal entries after a week, a month, a year, or a decade helps us see the hand of Christ at work in ways we often miss living day to day. The devil often uses the haunting lie that Christ doesn't assist His children. Our written accounts of His work in our lives say otherwise. Quiet writing helps us remember what God did for us.

Looking back later at our entries also points out our true goals and priorities in life as well as our areas of vulnerability and weakness. We will see the good along with the bad. This can assist us in keeping our goals and priorities centered on Christ and His will. It will also show us the areas of life where we need to ask for His help.

Leaving a written record of our spiritual journey also benefits our children and grandchildren as a legacy of our walk with God. I know that is Sue's motivation in writing to Mia. She wants to be sure Mia knows everything about her faith walk in case she does not have the time or opportunity to tell her. The record of our faithfulness will inspire the next generation to carry high the torch of godliness.

We have discussed the obvious ways of writing down our spiritual thoughts and insights in a journal book or on a computer. Besides these obvious ways, we could also write down observations from our spiritual journey

- In a Bible study notebook
- In the margins of our Bible
- In the margins of a book we are reading
- Through highlight markings in a book
- On note cards placed on a mirror or workstation and then later filed for future reference
- In e-mails to a trusted Christian friend
- In a photo album of significant spiritual events

Whatever method we use, our goal of recording our thoughts remains the same: to encounter Christ as we contemplate our journey together.

Day 10

Remember: Take time to record significant moments along your spiritual journey.

And Mary said: "My soul glorifies the Lord and my spirit rejoices in God my Savior" (Luke 1:46-47).

Day 11

QUIET SIMPLICITY

Then a teacher of the law came to him and said, "Teacher, I will follow you wherever you go." Jesus replied, "Foxes have holes and birds of the air have nests, but the Son of Man has no place to lay his head" (Matt. 8:19-20).

My wife and I chaperoned students on mission trips for the first 20 years of our employment at the university where we work. We visited every country in Central America except Nicaragua, several islands of the Caribbean, and four countries in South America. We worked in some countries more than once. Our son, Brent, accompanied us on most of those trips, so he started his world travels at nine years of age. He made friends in every country with the local children and still talks about them today.

We realized the impact the experiences had on him the Christmas following his first international trip. When we asked him what he wanted for Christmas, he replied, "Nothing. I have everything a kid needs." Pressing him to think of something served little purpose. Compared to his friends in Central America, he felt plenty blessed. Now don't get me wrong. He watched Saturday morning cartoons like every other kid did. So he knew the make and model of every new toy on the market. However, Brent decided at an early age that the accumulation of possessions served no worthy purpose in life. That lesson received reinforcement during his college experience when he spent the summer in India. That trip settled his value system for life.

In our Scripture reading for today, Jesus points out that He possessed very few of this world's material goods. He did not wear poverty as a badge or condemn the ownership of property. He merely observed that being His follower implies a life of simplicity. My Grandmother

Danley used to quote this verse of Scripture to us. I had no idea why at the time. I later realized she wanted to remind her grandchildren to avoid the trap of materialism. (I think she thought we had too many toys!)

I chose this passage for today because it illustrates the example Jesus set with His life. Perhaps the clearest admonition from His teachings came when He said, "Do not store up for yourselves treasures on earth, where moth and rust destroy, and where thieves break in and steal. But store up for yourselves treasures in heaven, where moth and rust do not destroy, and where thieves do not break in and steal. For where your treasure is, there your heart will be also" (6:19-21). Again, Jesus' words advise us to avoid the clutter of too many material possessions, which are only temporary, are subject to theft, and can distract us from what is really important. We must never define our personal worth by what we own. We find our true identity as children of God and citizens of His kingdom.

> *We find our true identity as children of God*
> *and citizens of His kingdom.*

The No. 1 spot in our value system should be Christ and His kingdom. Everything else must fall subject to Him. When we add up our life, Christ and His kingdom should be the only things that really matter.

Quiet simplicity invites us to meet with Christ in fresh ways as we loosen our grip on material things. It calls us to a life of generosity toward others and removes the trap of covetousness and envy. It untangles the complicated, distracted, and confusing schedule that materialism brings to our lives. It frees our time, energy, and effort for more productive and noble pursuits. It reduces our trips to the mall and slashes our purchasing for recreation or to impress neighbors. It reminds us to care for our delicate planet and teaches us to enjoy the simple pleasures in life, like a walk in the park, a sunset, or good conversation with a friend.

Quiet simplicity also includes avoiding certain things for a set time for spiritual purposes. We call this fasting. We can fast from certain kinds of food or portion sizes, all food, media, shopping, pleasures, luxuries, or just about anything else in order to present ourselves more fully to spiritual pursuits. When the Bible speaks of fasting, it usually refers to fasting from food. Jesus fasted from food for 40 days at the beginning of His public ministry (4:2). He assumed His followers would fast, for in Matt. 6:16 He said, *"When* you fast . . ."* (emphasis added). He also said fasting is a private matter between ourselves and God and not for public display (v. 18).

Jesus did not specify how often or how long we should fast; He did not want us to legalize the practice. We must always view it as a privilege of discipleship. The item we fast may be legitimate in and of itself. We abstain from it to loosen its hold on us and to remind us of our primary concern for Kingdom values. Our desire is to hunger as much for God as we do for food.

> "Let [a man], therefore, rejoice inwardly in his fasting in this very circumstance, that by his fasting he so turns away from the pleasure of the world as to be subject to Christ."
>
> —Augustine of Hippo (354–430)[8]

I can't really tell you how to apply the practice of quiet simplicity to your life. You'll find it a very personal matter. Only you know the things that matter most to you. Only you can hear what Christ says to you about them. You and He will work that out together as you talk with Him about each of your possessions, your lifestyle, and the things you love most. Jesus said it well, "Where your treasure is, there your heart will be also" (v. 21). Where is your heart? I assure you, wherever it is, you will meet Christ in fresh ways through quiet simplicity.

The truth of this lesson came home to me this spring when we moved my wife's folks from another state to our town. They had lived for 50 years in the house her dad built. The day for them to downsize arrived and everything was there, all laid out on garage sale tables—collections of tools, crafts, and household goods. A lifetime of collecting was over. Included were valuable items such as family photo albums and childhood artifacts. But it wasn't the value of the items that hit me; it was the certainty that someday I, too, would have to let go of everything. It was better for me to learn that lesson early and live by it than be caught off guard at life's end.

Practicing quiet simplicity helps us stay centered on what is most important. It is a practical way to keep Christ and His kingdom at the top of our treasure list. As we do it, we will find it to be another way to meet Christ and give our love to Him.

Day 11

Remember: Keep life simple.

Foxes have holes and birds of the air have nests,
but the Son of Man has no place to lay his head (Matt. 8:20).

Day 12

QUIET EXAMINATION

*Blessed are those who hunger and thirst for righteousness, for they will be filled. . . .
Blessed are the pure in heart, for they will see God* (Matt. 5:6, 8).

Every four years the world turns its attention to the international
Olympic Games. Athletes from across the globe compete for a gold,
silver, or bronze metal in the sport of their choice. Sports fans the
world over sit on the edge of their seats in front of television sets and
watch athletes represent their country. At the last Olympic Games one
television network broadcast 400 hours of Olympic programming on
6 satellite channels. Now that's great coverage! At the conclusion of
each athlete's performance, an international panel of judges rates it
with standardized criteria.

I've noticed from watching many Olympic events that athletes
usually rate their own performance the minute they complete it. Their
faces and body language tell the whole story. When the judges' ratings
appear on the scoreboard, athletes compare the judges' scores with
their own. The judges' scores seldom surprise the athletes.

This week we have explored our quiet time spent alone with
Christ. We characterized that time as an opportunity to be with the
One who loves us and whom we love in return. Words need not be
spoken and deeds need not be performed for us to enjoy our fellowship with Christ. However, spiritual growth and development occur
most often when we organize our time into a few basic practices.
These practices include prayer, listening, reading the Bible and other
Christian books, thinking reflectively, writing down our thoughts,
and maintaining a lifestyle of simplicity.

rendezvous

*Words need not be spoken and deeds need not be performed
for us to enjoy our fellowship with Christ.*

Today wraps up our exploration of our quiet time alone with
Christ. We want to conclude this week by considering one more quiet
practice—examination. Examination offers us an opportunity to do
what Olympic athletes do, that is, rate our day, our mood, our feelings, our goals, our priorities, our spiritual progress, or our life. It creates time and space for us to reflect on spiritual matters and gives
Christ an open door to talk to us about them.

This practice may be conducted daily, weekly, or occasionally.
Many Christians conclude every day by asking a series of questions on
which they rate themselves. Changing the questions periodically
keeps the practice from becoming stale and routine. Daily questions
could include such things as these:

- Did I set aside time today to pray, listen to Christ, and read the
  Bible?
- Did I talk to Christ conversationally throughout the day?
- Did I direct my public conversation and action toward the glory
  of God?
- Did I attempt to do good to all people and in all situations?
- Did I thank God for the good gifts I enjoyed?

Dozens of other questions could be considered according to each
one's particular spiritual journey. These simply illustrate the direction
such questions might take.

We could ask ourselves additional examination questions every
Sunday or on the last Sunday of each month. Here are some possibilities:

- Did I take time to think about my spiritual journey and mentally process what Christ is saying to me?
- Did I take time to write down spiritual insights, questions,
  prayer requests, or thoughts about what Christ is teaching me?

62

- Have I lived in a manner that aims toward simplicity?
- Have I read a Christian book or given myself to studying about God or my spiritual journey?
- Am I on target with the goals Christ has given me for my life?

Entire books have been written on the Christian practice of examination, so I will not take time to explore every facet of it here. John Wesley used the classic *The Imitation of Christ* by Thomas à Kempis for spiritual examination. I have found this book helpful for my spiritual journey.

In our Bible reading for today, Jesus presented a series of conditions that God blesses. I have selected two of them for our consideration; they relate well to the practice of examination. In verse 6 He said the Father will fill those who hunger and thirst after righteousness. I don't know about you, but when I'm hungry or thirsty, nothing else matters. The drive for food or water consumes every thought. Likewise, the Father will not give us spiritual growth and maturity in our sleep. If a desire to be a committed follower of Christ consumes our every thought, He will honor that hunger with spiritual fullness. In verse 8 Jesus said the Father will show himself to all who have a single eye on Him and His kingdom. We will see glimpses of God every day and spend eternity with Him in heaven.

The practice of quiet examination fosters our hunger and thirst for righteousness and helps keep our hearts pure before God. It gives Christ an opportunity to talk to us about our day—the things we said or didn't say, the ways we reacted, the feelings we had, and the body language we used. Quiet examination also teaches us to monitor our own physical and emotional systems. We can take note of the things that irritate us, bring us stress, put a knot in our stomach, or cause us to grieve. We can also reflect on the things that bring us pleasure, joy, hope, or determination.

Through quiet examination we can name our successes and failures. Our successes we can commit to Christ as a love offering that He might use to help others in Kingdom work. Our failures we can confess humbly, and then we can pray for growth to do better in the future. We can present all of our feelings and reactions to Christ and let Him help us sort through them and decide where to go with them. Above all, we can use quiet examination as a time to depend more completely on Christ, come to terms with our weaknesses, and capitalize on our strengths.

The practice of quiet examination fosters our hunger and thirst for righteousness, and it helps us keep our hearts pure before God.

We need annual physical checkups to make sure our bodies are in good working order. We also get our car engines and tires checked regularly. I bought a new lawn mower this spring. It has an hour meter mounted near the engine so I can have the machine checked at regular intervals. With so much attention to checkups in life, doesn't it make sense that we should provide regular maintenance to our spiritual lives? Daily, weekly, or monthly examinations can provide that maintenance and give us an additional opportunity to meet with Christ.

I heard a minister say something in my teen years that has impressed me for a lifetime. He said, "For the believer who is spiritually sensitive, there will be no surprises on Judgment Day." Until that moment I assumed that Judgment Day would be like a television game show. The winners (those who inherited heaven) would be totally surprised and amazed at God's mercy. I've come to understand the minister's point. If we practice quiet examination, the Holy Spirit will be faithful to work with us daily to get and keep our spiritual house in order. In the end, the last examination will come as no big surprise. He's been prepping us for that day throughout life!

Put into regular practice the ways we have discussed this week for encountering Christ in your life. Remember, you participate in these practices not to punch your spiritual performance card but to enjoy your love affair with Christ. You should anxiously anticipate your rendezvous with Him.

Day 12

Remember: Take time to examine your life.

Blessed are those who hunger and thirst for righteousness, for they will be filled. . . . Blessed are the pure in heart, for they will see God (Matt. 5:6, 8).

"Friendship is one species of love; and is, in its proper sense, a disinterested reciprocal love between two persons. . . . The properties of Christian friendship are the same as the properties of love; with those which St. Paul so beautifully describes in the thirteenth chapter of the first Epistle to the Corinthians. And it produces, as occasions offer, every good word and work."

—John Wesley (1703-91)[9]

ENCOUNTERING CHRIST
IN MY CLOSEST
RELATIONSHIPS

rendezvous

Day 13

A FRIEND FOR ALL TIMES

As Jesus was walking beside the Sea of Galilee, he saw two brothers, Simon called Peter and his brother Andrew. They were casting a net into the lake, for they were fishermen. "Come, follow me," Jesus said, "and I will make you fishers of men." At once they left their nets and followed him (Matt. 4:18-20).

Christ has blessed my life with a partner for the journey. Sue and I share everything from the high and holy moments of ministry to an occasional chili dog at Sonic. I couldn't ask for anyone to care more about me or look after my well-being. She always believes in me and is always there for me. She's my soul mate for life. I also share my personal and spiritual journey with Gary, my best friend. He listens to my problems, acts as a sounding board for my half-cooked ideas, and provides me with spiritual advice. I'd trust Gary with my wallet and my life.

Today's Scripture reading reminds us that Jesus lived His life on this earth and conducted His ministry in companionship. We just heard Him call Peter to be His disciple. What a privilege Peter enjoyed sharing such an intimate journey with the Master. They experienced many high and low moments together. On nearly every significant occasion in Jesus' public ministry, we see Peter right at Jesus' side. I think Peter needed Jesus more than Jesus needed Peter. However, Jesus placed a high value on journeying together in life with a trusted friend. He left us an essential example to follow.

God created us for relationship. That's why prisoners in solitary confinement lose touch with reality and why survivors on desert islands talk to volleyballs, as we discussed on Day 6. God made us in His image, His Trinitarian image. So He always lives and acts from a shared perspective. We, too, have an interdependent nature. But we also need regular times of solitude. We spent last week looking at a few ways we encounter Christ in these solitary times. We need private time alone with Him to regroup and nourish our relationship. The time comes, however, when we need to leave our private sanctuary and return to the give-and-take of society.

God created us for relationship.

Few of us live alone as cave dwellers. Few of us live in the cloistered environment of a monastery. Most of us have jobs, responsibilities, and families in a fast-paced world with other people. This week we want to explore a few of the many ways we can encounter Christ and grow spiritually with someone who is close to us. We do not have to leave Christ in our quiet place; He will go with us as we share our lives with others. Our spiritual journey can find enrichment and Christ can reveal himself in a special way when we are in the company of a trusted mate or friend.

We often call this trusted mate or friend an accountability partner. This person need not fill out an application or have certain qualifications. He or she just needs a good set of ears, a growing relationship with Christ, some time, and lots of patience and understanding. You can talk regularly and share your faith walk with an accountability partner. It will add a new dimension to the relationship you share with Jesus Christ.

Believing husbands and wives should always share their faith together. Most Christians also find it beneficial to have a friend of the same gender with whom they can relate. I often need to get a man's opinion from Gary or have him challenge me as only another man can do. Sue does the same thing with a trusted female accountability partner.

The ground rules for this spiritual relationship require both parties to be open, honest, and vulnerable with one another. The minute

I approach the subject of being open, honest, and vulnerable with another person, especially someone other than a mate, defenses go up and ears shut down. That can be scary business! Being vulnerable can be threatening; admitting weaknesses, bad feelings, and failures can be hard; and being put on the spot to give an account of our choices can be embarrassing. Admitting we need help (sometimes lots of it) can cause us to feel less than victorious. This is especially true if you are a man like me. I don't like to admit I get lost when driving or that I need the direction sheet to put something new together. It's a guy thing! Sharing your spiritual journey with an accountability partner takes valuable time and requires effort to schedule. You'll also find it takes emotional energy.

So, yes, there's a price to pay to have the trust level high enough for spiritual accountability to work well. Nevertheless, the benefits outweigh the costs. First, we often see ourselves in a more idealized way than others do. This trusted friend helps us see our blind spots. We get a truer picture of ourselves, without our own self-justification. Second, an accountability partner can help form us into better Christians. This person regularly holds us accountable for our spiritual commitments and responsibilities. Third, this person helps us think through and test ideas before we implement them. That, in and of itself, is worth our time. Just having someone ask, "Have you thought of this?" can save us from certain embarrassment and sometimes failure. Fourth, this person forces us to be totally open and honest about our spiritual walk with Christ. That, in turn, helps us face the reality of who we are as a Christian. Finally, and best of all, this person keeps pointing us in the direction of God and His plans for life.

Spiritual companionship with a mate or trusted friend can be an incredible channel for Christ to work. It adds depth and breadth to the spiritual exercises we presented last week. We become coworkers with our accountability partner in tracking each other's spiritual journey. We have someone to encourage us through difficult times, someone to challenge us to victory in times of temptation, and someone to help us hold on when we are most ready to give up.

> "We must pray for one another, helping one another up with a tender hand if there has been any slip or fall."
> —Isaac Penington (1617-80)[10]

In time, we may find we experience Christ's love and direction more completely with the aid of a spiritual friend than we would if we tried to live life by ourselves.

Day 13

Remember: Our spiritual journey finds enrichment in the company of a trusted mate or friend that can be found in no other setting.

As Jesus was walking beside the Sea of Galilee, he saw two brothers, Simon called Peter and his brother Andrew (Matt. 4:18).

Day 14

AN AMAZING THING HAPPENS

For where two or three come together in my name,
there am I with them (Matt. 18:20).

I mentioned Superman and the Lone Ranger on Day 3. I knew both of them pretty well as a kid. We met together every Saturday morning at the black-and-white television set. For a long time I idolized my heroes for being rugged individualists who lived life on their own terms and answered to no one. Then one day a startling truth hit me. They weren't loners after all. Superman worked closely with Lois Lane and Jimmy Olson. The Lone Ranger traveled with Tonto. I guess even superheroes need coworkers!

Today as we continue to explore ways Christ meets us with a trusted friend, I want us to look back over the practices of last week and pick a few to reconsider. This time we will view them as a shared activity. It always amazes me how the same activity takes on a different feel when shared with a friend.

Everything we do together in His name assumes a different texture because we are doing it with a friend and not by ourselves.

In our Bible reading for today, Jesus made a startling revelation about His followers getting together. He said anytime just two of them meet as believers for spiritual purposes an amazing thing happens. He comes to be right there with them. Isn't that incredible! I have Christian friends who leave an empty chair when they meet simply to remind them that Jesus sits right there with them. Everything we do together in His name assumes a different texture because we are doing it with a friend and not by ourselves. Just look at the way this works with some of the practices from last week.

Prayer. We pray together with a friend for many reasons. Sometimes we worship and praise God together. Sometimes we pray together about our problems, crises, or concerns. Sometimes we pray for strength for a task or victory against temptation. Sometimes we band together for the needs of others or our broken and hurting world. Regardless of the reason that unites us in prayer, a special time of fellowship with Christ always accompanies our effort. We may not always sense His presence, but God's Word reminds us that He is present nonetheless.

Taking the responsibility to pray privately for our own needs and to nurture our soul in a personal relationship with Christ marks a growing believer. However, we also need others to share in our prayer lives. Saying "I need you to pray with me" to a trusted friend reminds us that we really do need each other. It requires humility to admit we need the assistance of another in our lives.

Listening. Sometimes all talking ceases, and we sit quietly together with Christ and our friend. This most often occurs at the end of prayer. Christ has a way of saying just the right thing in those quiet moments. Sometimes He speaks words in our hearts; sometimes He floods us with an assurance that He is with us, has heard our prayer, and is going to take care of us and the situation we currently face.

In the days that follow our prayer together, the devil often tempts us to believe that Christ is not with us, that He has not heard our prayer, and that our situation is not under Christ's control. We can remind ourselves in those doubting moments that our friend listened with us; we have a witness that we heard it right! Oh the assurance that comes from having a friend testify with us that God is in control.

Bible study. We must study the Bible personally for spiritual growth and development. However, studying alone is never enough. We must get together with a friend and receive confirmation on thoughts or interpretations we have on Scripture.

I always feel reassured when flying to know that after the pilot goes through a checklist of the aircraft's equipment prior to takeoff, the copilot looks over the same checklist. Flight attendants do the same with cabin doors and locks. They check then cross-check them. Studying the Bible with a friend gives us a cross-check that we're reading and understanding it correctly. We might even see things in Scripture when reading it with a friend that we wouldn't see otherwise. I don't know how that happens, but I know it's true.

Thinking. Along with a shared Bible study, it's also important to have a sounding board for our thoughts. My friend Gary logs many hours listening to me wax on and on about thoughts I've been having regarding God's work in our world or what God is doing in a particular situation. Sometimes Gary says, "I think you're right." Sometimes I get, "I don't know about that." Sometimes he comes back with, "Absolutely no way."

God does not entrust any of us with all truth. He alone has that privilege. So we need to get together and put each of our pieces of knowledge on the table to see images form. It's like a treasure hunter with half of a map to buried treasure searching for the person with the other half. Once they find each other and put the two map pieces together, they can locate the buried treasure. The same is often true with truths found in God's Word.

God does not entrust any of us with all truth.

Examination. Examination is an important personal exercise. Only we know what's in the depths of our heart, and only we know if we're being honest with our answers. We're the only ones besides Christ who really know ourselves. Having said that, it's also true that examination takes on an important new dimension when practiced with a friend. One way to do this is to have our friend ask us a series of questions about our spiritual journey that we will then answer honestly. Saints through the ages have practiced examination in this way to their spiritual benefit.

You know how the mind works. We're not as likely to take an extra helping of mashed potatoes or a slice of pie if we know we're going to have to report it to a dieting partner. I've said "No thank you" to more than one tempting lunch dessert simply because I didn't want to confess to my wife that I ate something that wasn't good for me. Likewise, spiritual temptation may lose some of its appeal if we're accountable to another person for our choices. We will probably be more careful in our daily walk if we know a friend is going to ask us about it.

This certainly does not exhaust all of the ways you and a trusted friend can apply the practices we discussed last week. However, I hope this gives you a flavor of what's available for you as you meet Christ with a friend. Think about these five practices today and imagine ways you can incorporate them into your time together with your accountability partner. As you do this, you will begin to encounter Christ in new ways.

Day 14

Remember: When you get together with another believer, Jesus joins you.

For where two or three come together in my name, there am I with them (Matt. 18:20).

Day 15

IN CONTROL

But he walked right through the crowd and went on his way (Luke 4:30).

I'm greeted every morning as I drive to work with the same sight: pairs of people walking through the neighborhood or on the walking trail near our home—two women, two men, a husband and wife, two mothers pushing baby carriages. They're always talking together; they actually look like they're enjoying themselves.

This scene reminds me that whether it's walking for exercise, working out at the gym, or counting calories on a diet, we accomplish the task better with a partner. Let's face it, getting dressed every day to exercise regardless of the weather requires discipline and determination. Such discipline and determination come easier when supported by another person. Plus, having some company along the walking path adds interest and variety. This principle holds as true with the Christian walk as it does for dieting and exercise.

Today we're going to look at the necessity of exercising discipline in a variety of areas. We seldom find discipline easy, but it may be easier when shared with a friend. Growing in Christ requires us to bring every part of our lives under His Lordship and control. Paul said, "I beat my body and make it my slave so that after I have preached to others, I myself will not be disqualified for the prize" (1 Cor. 9:27). Living a life of discipline opens new doors for Christ to work in and through us. Without a doubt, each of the following areas is personal and challenging. We can master and control them with the help of the Holy Spirit, but the task becomes easier with the support and assistance of a friend. Let's consider a few areas where we must exercise discipline in our lives:

Our speech. The Hebrew people in Bible times believed that once spoken, words took on a life of their own. They could never be called back; their effect could never be neutralized. They believed care should be taken when speaking words, because they have great power to both create and destroy. A person's words live on long after he or she goes to the grave. What's more, our words testify clearly to what's really in the heart. So great care must be exercised to avoid criticizing, complaining, critiquing, yelling, cursing, gossiping, slandering, and backbiting with other people.

In today's Bible reading, Jesus found himself in a difficult situation with the hometown crowd. His observations on the Scripture reading for the day and its relation to His own life and ministry so enraged them that they plotted to kill Him. The crowd left the synagogue and relocated to a nearby hill where they planned to throw Jesus to His death. Luke says Jesus walked away from the highly charged scene and took His ministry elsewhere.

You've heard the phrase "Let's take this outside" spoken when two people are close to settling their differences with their fists. Jesus certainly could have taken on the crowd of hometown folks—and beaten the entire group—but He didn't. He controlled His speech and His emotions; He walked away from a fight. Jesus provides a worthy example for us to follow when anger flairs. Christ wants us to use our speech to speak words of blessing, truth, encouragement, forgiveness, and love. A gentle word from a friend combined with the Holy Spirit's touch can remind us to use our words with the same care Christ used His.

Our bodies. We must learn to control our physical desires. One of the hazards of living in a developed nation is the false expectation that we can satisfy our every possible desire. A student once confessed to me that he believed he would die if he could not indulge in premarital sex. Now you and I both know celibacy is not fatal, but this young man convinced himself it was! Delayed gratification was just not part of his thinking.

Every physical craving we have must be cross-checked with Scripture to test its validity. Then we must learn to moderate our desires. This includes limiting the food we eat and the portions we take. It means monitoring everything from soft drinks to prescription medications. Nothing is more frightening or dangerous than letting our bodies control us. Companioning with a close friend can help us gain control of our appetites. His or her watchful eyes can reinforce the quiet voice of the Holy Spirit.

> "But sometimes, indeed, it is necessary to use force, to resist the sensual appetite bravely, to take no heed of what the flesh likes, and what it dislikes; but to take every care to bring it even unwillingly under the sway of the spirit."
>
> —Thomas à Kempis[11]

Our moods. Each of us has a unique way of responding to life. It's like having an emotional fingerprint. Some have wide mood swings; others have hardly a ripple from day to day. Some see the bright side of everything; others see only dark clouds. A part of the maturing process for every follower of Jesus Christ is learning to control these emotional highs and lows. With the Holy Spirit's help we must learn to master them so we can represent Christ in the best possible way. That's where a mature friend's perceptive words can be a great help. He or she can expose us to a broader and more balanced view of life. This will allow the Holy Spirit more room to help us control our emotional responses. The broader our outlook, the better our response.

Our material possessions. We devoted Day 11 to simplicity. We discussed limiting our material possessions and loosening our grip on things of this world. A trusted friend, such as a spouse or accountability partner, can assist us in avoiding materialism and excess in our lives. Honestly answering the question "Do I really need that?" can help us separate our wants from our actual needs.

Our care for the earth. God placed Adam and Eve in the Garden of Eden and made them caretakers of His wonderful creation (Gen. 1:28; 2:15). People used to consider nature indestructible and natural resources limitless. We now know better. Global warming and resource depletion have given us early warning signs that we must change our ways to survive on earth. We must remember that earth does not belong to us; it belongs to God. He has entrusted us with this special gift and expects us to take care of it.

Proper care of the earth is a way to show our love for God and the future generations who will inherit what we leave behind. Few people find this easy to master. That's why we need a friend to hold us accountable to it. Walking or riding a bike, rather than driving; using energy wisely; recycling, not littering—all of these are ways to thank God for the gift of His good earth.

Think of what you can do to practice discipline in your life and share this with your friend or accountability partner. With the help of the Holy Spirit and the support of your friend, you will have ample resources to master the different areas of your life. As you do, don't be surprised when Christ meets you amid your faithful efforts and blesses and invigorates you with His love.

Day 15

Remember: Remind yourself daily to live a life that is in control.
But he walked right through the crowd and went on his way (Luke 4:30).

Day 16

DROP AND GIVE ME FIVE

"Abba, Father," he said, "everything is possible for you. Take this cup from me. Yet not what I will, but what you will" (Mark 14:36).

A student walked into my office one day and made a statement that forever changed my view of student-professor relationships. This happened during my early days as a university professor. Following class that day, this young man stepped into my doorway and said, "I disagree with what you said in class today. I think you need to reconsider your position." The student was not being disrespectful. He simply wanted me to add his view to my class presentation.

I at first wanted to ignore him. After all, a professor is supposed to know more about the subject than a junior-level student. But instead I chose to thank him for his insight and candor. In all honesty, once I thought about what he said, I realized he had a point. My student taught me a lesson in submission.

Discussions of spiritual submission have fallen on hard times these days. The doctrine of the priesthood of all believers is often misunderstood. Many well-meaning Christians think it means that every believer is on his or her own and is responsible to no one. Not so. Christianity is more about community and submitting to one another. The minute someone uses the word *submission,* our minds immediately jump to worst-case scenarios like these:

- Submissive wives under the domination of overbearing or abusive husbands
- Military recruits ordered by harsh drill sergeants to "drop and give me five"

- Social doormats who think they are nobodies without any worth

But this is nothing at all like the biblical meaning of submission.

God is himself a community—a Trinity of persons who mutually submit to each other within the Godhead. Examples abound from Jesus' life and ministry of Him submitting to His Father. Perhaps the best-known example occurs in the Bible lesson for today. As Jesus prayed in the Garden of Gethsemane, He saw the upcoming events of His passion. We will never know what He saw that night. But whatever He saw was horrific. His natural tendency shied away from it. Nevertheless, He overcame that tendency and submitted to His Father's will. We are eternally grateful to Him, for through His submission He saved us from sin. Praise His name!

> "The Christian way is different . . . Christ says 'Give me All. I don't want so much of your time and so much of your money and so much of your work: I want You. . . . No half-measures are any good.'"
> —C. S. Lewis (1898—1963)[12]

While discussing the Holy Spirit, Jesus mentioned some of the ways the Spirit submits to Him. For example, Jesus said the Spirit will testify about Jesus (John 15:26). He "will not speak on his own; he will speak only what he hears" (16:13). The Son submitting to the Father and the Spirit submitting to the Son remind us that the persons of the Trinity submit to each other out of love. We, too, must learn to submit to one another the way God does within the Trinity.

We first of all must submit to God and His plan for our lives. You probably know the first spiritual law from Campus Crusade for Christ by heart: "God loves you and has a wonderful plan for your life." Submission to that plan leads to our salvation. Beyond that we submit to God daily as we learn to follow the lead of His Spirit. He leads us so we can be part of His plan to renew the world and save all who will accept His offer of salvation. That notion of submission may be easy to grasp.

It may be harder, however, to accept the notion of submitting to a fellow believer, as I found myself doing with my student. Paul put it like this, "Submit to one another out of reverence for Christ" (Eph. 5:21). From that statement Paul launched into a discussion of submission within three relationships: husbands and wives, parents and children, masters and slaves. For an in-depth look at this passage and Paul's thoughts on submission, you may want to consult a commentary or Bible study book.

Submission is included in a week that highlights encountering Christ in our closest relationships because that's where we tend to understand and exercise it best. We may submit to those in authority at church or work out of obligation or self-preservation. But only within a nurturing, trusting relationship can we understand and practice genuine biblical submission. With a friend we can discover together God's will and direction as we submit to our friend's instruction or correction.

A genuine spiritual friend may call us to submission while

- Discipling us, as in "Read John 14—16 and describe how the Spirit wants to work in your life."
- Teaching us, as in "Here is what this passage of Scripture means."
- Correcting us, as in "You were wrong in what you said. You should apologize to her."
- Guiding us, as in "You should take a long weekend to pray and fast for God's direction in this matter."

Only we can decide if we will allow ourselves to be taught, corrected, and guided. We must be willing to submit to our friend.

Christ often meets with us in this setting because He can work through a humble and teachable spirit. This spirit allows Christ to speak through our friend's insights and experiences. We can learn spiritual truths that will come our way through no other means. Freedom and release come when we realize we don't have to bear the burden of being right all of the time. We can be at ease knowing we don't have the only way of looking at a matter. Admitting we are not on our own but need the instruction of others also is quite freeing. Thus you find liberation in learning from your friend.

Weekly I deal with problems on the job that result when one Christian believer does not submit to another. Sometimes the issues are institutional, involving the chain of command. But usually the problems are relational, with personality and human pride hindering one believer from teaching another.

Yes, this is a tough practice to implement. No, it may never be popular. Nonetheless all serious disciples of Jesus must learn to submit to one another for their soul's comfort and joy. The Trinitarian Godhead practices it, and so must we. Think throughout this day of practical ways you can submit to your accountability partner. As you put submission into practice, you will encounter Christ in ways you have never encountered Him before.

Day 16

Remember: You must learn to submit to one another out of reverence for Christ.

Not what I will, but what you will (Mark 14:36).

Day 17

SIMON SAYS

This is to my Father's glory, that you bear much fruit,
showing yourselves to be my disciples (John 15:8).

Sue and I have invested our time and lives in mentoring young people. We first mentored them in the youth groups of the churches we pastored. This, no doubt, influenced us to shift our ministry to the university setting where we have spent more than two decades working with young people. Mentoring takes time, patience, and perseverance. Both the mentor and the one being mentored must commit to the process and work at it for the long haul.

The rewards of mentoring a younger Christian defy description. Many are like those that parents receive raising their children. Seeing a fellow believer in Jesus Christ grow and mature in the faith carries eternal benefits. It is a work done here on earth that Paul said meets us on the other side (1 Cor. 3:10-15). Sue and I receive Christmas cards with family pictures and updates from students we have mentored across the past two decades. What a blessing! Some of our students have already crossed over to their heavenly reward and now cheer us on as we continue the journey here on earth.

The rewards of mentoring a younger Christian defy description.

Jesus taught His disciples in John 15 about the spiritual pruning and growth they needed for them to develop as disciples. Read this instruction in verses 1-17. Our verse for today represents one thought from this discussion. This instruction reminds us we must mentor young believers so they can grow and develop as disciples of Jesus

85

Christ. Mature Christians mentoring younger ones has a long tradition. When we mentor another believer, we are carrying on this tradition that began with Jesus himself.

Mentoring happens within relationships. Through a relationship we guide another believer in the faith and knowledge of Jesus Christ, as well as the Christian lifestyle. You present and model lessons, and your friend learns them one at a time through the give-and-take of ordinary life.

Who can be a mentor? Anyone with knowledge of the Bible and experience in the faith can be one. Age plays little role in being a mentor. We usually think of a mentor as an older person, but that need not be the case. Peers can perform the task just as well. An accountability partner can mentor a young person. Parents can mentor their children and other young people their children's ages. Married couples can mentor other couples, either younger or the same age. Teachers can mentor students, as Sue and I do. The combination of possibilities is almost endless.

Mentorship can include studying a Christian book or the Bible together, praying together, talking about life issues or lifestyle choices, or being accountable to another person. It can also involve working side-by-side in a ministry assignment, on a mission trip, or at an evangelism activity. Just about any setting or task can serve the purpose of training, equipping, and encouraging a young believer to grow in the faith and knowledge of Jesus Christ.

No matter who mentors or how it's done, the Holy Spirit plays the most vital role in discipling a younger believer. The Spirit reaches within the disciple's heart and brings spiritual truths to life so they can be lived out daily.

Another important thing about mentoring is that the young disciple sees in the mentor's life a flesh-and-blood example of what is being taught. Paul referred to this when he said, "Follow my example, as I follow the example of Christ" (1 Cor. 11:1). Remember the childhood game Simon Says? Children play the game by doing whatever the leader does when he or she says "Simon says." You don't do what the leader does until you hear those words. In mentoring, the leader never gets a day off. A mentor can never say, "Do as I say and not as I do." His or her life remains Exhibit No. 1 for Christianity. Mentors always know that the young disciple follows close behind. It's an awesome responsibility and an awesome privilege at the same time.

Why should we be mentors? First and foremost because Jesus instructs us to help make disciples (Matt. 28:19-20). Beyond that, we will receive an incredible sense of satisfaction by investing in another believer. It's wonderful to watch a young disciple grow and develop in the faith and knowledge of Christ. Third, mentoring gives us a chance to pass on what has been given to us. Very few believers are self-made. Most had mentors and encouragers along the way who parented them to maturity in the faith. Fourth, it helps us become lifelong learners. Working with another believer keeps us on our toes and sharpens our skills at answering the tough questions about the faith and practice of Christianity.

> "It is very important for us to associate with others who are walking in the right way. . . . Those who have drawn close to God have the ability to bring us closer to him, for in a sense they take us with them."
> —Teresa of Ávila (1515-82)[13]

I still remember the two big "But why?" phases of my son's upbringing. The first occurred at about 3 years of age, the second at about 13. I think the second one proved harder than the first. I wanted to say "Just because" to his endless string of questions, but I didn't. I forced myself to develop reasonable answers. This postmodern generation asks "But why?" more than any in a long time. They deserve well-reasoned answers. They will be nurtured in faith, and we will grow with the exercise.

This week we are looking at ways we encounter Christ with those closest to us. As with the other ways we have discussed, Christ comes uniquely to us while mentoring disciples. There's just something special about investing time and energy in another person that can be found in no other experience. Try it and see what I mean!

Day 17

Remember: You can participate in the incredible responsibility and privilege of mentoring a disciple for Christ.

This is to my Father's glory, that you bear much fruit, showing yourselves to be my disciples (John 15:8).

Day 18

BECAUSE WE CARE

Then Jesus went around teaching from village to village.
Calling the Twelve to him, he sent them out two by two and
gave them authority over evil spirits (Mark 6:6-7).

Mattie Belle worked as the president's secretary at the university Sue and I attended. She worked hard for the president all week, then loaded 20 students in four cars every other Friday afternoon for weekend services at churches within driving distance of the campus. She called the group the Circuit Riders because they traveled from church to church like preachers of the old West. Sue and I met while serving together with the Circuit Riders. We have some great memories from these group adventures.

Mattie Belle poured much of her time and energy into that ministry. I'm sure people found spiritual help in the hundreds of services conducted by the Circuit Riders over the years. But Mattie Belle's greater contribution to the Kingdom may have been her investment in the lives of the student team members. She wasn't just a staff sponsor; she was a combination mother, nurturer, counselor, matchmaker, and life coach. She poured her life into us. Many of us serve in ministry today because of her confidence in us. What an example she gave us of both service and ministry. I'm sure she did it because she cared— about us and God's work.

In our Bible reading for today, Jesus sent His disciples on a ministry assignment. Notice how they went out: two by two. The Bible abounds with examples of ministry being conducted by believers working in pairs. Paul and Barnabas, Paul and Silas, Barnabas and Mark, Priscilla and Aquila—all worked side by side in ministry. So on a week when we are talking about practices done with someone close to us, how fitting that we include ministry and service as two of those practices.

The Bible abounds with examples of ministry being conducted by believers working in pairs.

Jesus said a great deal about service during His earthly ministry. In Luke 22:27 He said, "For who is greater, the one who is at the table or the one who serves? Is it not the one who is at the table? But I am among you as one who serves." He modeled servanthood for His disciples by washing their feet at His Last Supper with them. During that sacred event He said, "I tell you the truth, no servant is greater than his master, nor is a messenger greater than the one who sent him" (John 13:16). Jesus modeled a life of service; we must follow His example.

Although Christian service and ministry may be performed alone, they assume an added dimension when shared with another. That's why Jesus sent His disciples out in pairs. Service and ministry put feet to our shared faith. In a very real sense we become Christ's hands and feet to continue His ministry to needy and hurting people. We become the channel God chooses to use in reaching out to those who need Him most. We can usually do that best with a fellow worker at our side.

In Gen. 18 God promised to bless the inhabitants of the earth through the family line of Abraham. Something went terribly wrong with that intention. God intended to bless the Hebrew people, and they in turn were to bless their neighbors. They interpreted their blessings as privilege and not responsibility. Very little has changed from that time until now. God still intends to bless Christ's followers so they in turn can bless their neighbors. But if we're not careful, we, too, can falsely interpret our God-sent blessings as privilege and not responsibility. This makes service and ministry vitally important in our Christian walk.

Service and ministry offer our time, energy, effort, concern, money, and influence to people we know who need help. It means being available when it's convenient and when it's not. Service and ministry take us out of our comfort zone for short or long periods of time. We do not serve and minister out of obligation or expectation. We do not do these things to feel good about ourselves or better than those who do not do them. We serve and minister because

- We genuinely care about people.
- We see people as God sees them.
- We really love others.
- We want justice in our world.
- God's love for us must flow forth in love for others.

We all have different ages, abilities, skills, personalities, and interests, but God has a place of service or a ministry for everyone. When Sue and I took students on annual mission trips, the team consisted of different persons with different abilities. Yet each year when everyone did his or her part, no matter how small it seemed, we got the job done—together. And we had a great deal of fun while doing it.

In Matt. 25:31-46 Jesus discussed the Day of Judgment. He said everyone would be judged on that day—both righteous and unrighteous. God will make eternal decisions about our relationship with Him and our faith from the deeds we did on earth. Jesus named such things as feeding the hungry, giving a drink to the thirsty, caring for strangers, sharing clothes, and visiting the sick or imprisoned. He added that we perform these services for God when we do them for anyone we know in need. That opens wide the door for us to serve or minister to anyone with whom we come in contact. Each of us will stand at the judgment, but we may find we do a better job of serving others by doing it with a friend.

Service and ministry—these are two important practices of Christian discipleship. Like Mattie Belle, we do it because we care. We care about people, and we care about God's work. Get with your friend today and find a ministry you can do together. Be accountable to one another. Remember, when you serve and minister, you might just encounter Christ in the eyes of those in need. So encourage each other to do your best. Your efforts will help others, you'll be helping in the Lord's work, and you will probably enjoy yourself—especially if you meet the One you love.

Day 18

Remember: Service and ministry can often be conducted best with the assistance of a friend.

He sent them out two by two (Mark 6:7).

Day 19

NEVER FORSAKEN

About the ninth hour Jesus cried out in a loud voice,
"Eloi, Eloi, lama sabachthani?"—which means, "My God, my God,
why have you forsaken me?" (Matt. 27:46).

Kevin and Janell attended our Sunday School class for many years. They made it to class every Sunday and participated in all of the class's social activities and service projects. Then Kevin began having seizures again. I say again because he'd had them five years earlier due to a brain tumor. Kevin improved following treatment at that time and resumed life with an adjusted schedule. With the return of the seizures, he faced another grueling regimen of treatments and a series of surgeries. The surgeries and treatments stretched over the next seven and a half years.

Throughout this entire ordeal, Janell stood by his bedside, took him to doctor's appointments, and cared for his every need. Kevin may have had the physical problem, but Kevin and Janell went through the valley of suffering together. They bore the burden of this affliction as a team. In the end we lost Kevin. We all learned valuable lessons about the companionship of suffering as we watched these two journey together down that road.

Today we conclude our look at Christian practices done with someone close to us. We end this week with a look at suffering and how we can meet intimately with Christ in the midst of it. Suffering is never a pleasant subject to discuss. We'd just as soon avoid talking about it and experiencing it. We never have to go looking for suffering; it always finds us no matter where we live, who we are, or what we do for a living. No amount of power, education, fame, prestige, or

93

money can isolate us from suffering. It is the common lot of every traveler of this world.

> *No amount of power, education, fame, prestige,*
> *or money can isolate us from suffering.*

God-followers since the days of Job have known the heartaches as well as the benefits of suffering. Job's experience reminds us that suffering can be a good disciple-making tool. We hate to agree but know it's true. Suffering can actually make us better in this life and prepare our souls for eternity. It can grow our faith and draw us closer to Christ. When we look back over a difficult time in life, we often see that Christ either walked beside us—or carried us—through the difficulty. Christ can meet us and draw us close to His side in times of suffering in ways we might otherwise miss.

Our Scripture passage for today gives us Christ's words as He hung on the Cross. These words remind us that Christ suffered while on earth. This certainly was not the only time He suffered while living with us. He suffered frequently at the hands of the devil, who often tempted Him to use His divine power for personal needs, to impress a crowd, or to compromise with evil. See Matt. 4:1-11, Mark 1:12-13, or Luke 4:1-13 for early examples of these temptations. He suffered frequently at the hands of the religious leaders who tried to trick Him or discredit His ministry (11:37-54). He suffered frequently with His disciples who failed again and again to understand who He was, why He came, and what the kingdom of God on earth was all about (Matt. 16:21-23; 20:20-28). Today's scripture is just one example of the many ways Jesus suffered.

If we could script our lives, we would no doubt write suffering completely out of the script. But we're not given the chance to do that. Some suffer more than others, but all suffer at one level or another. For some it's a physical burden, for others the burden can be psychological, emotional, or relational. Added to this is the suffering caused by accidents. Natural disasters such as volcanic eruptions, tornados, hurricanes, and tsunamis visit every continent of the world. Good people suffer and die in all sorts of tragic circumstances.

A silver lining surrounds the dark cloud of suffering when a friend joins us and shares the experience. Maybe you have a friend who is suffering. You have the privilege of standing beside him or her through these difficult times. You may be called upon to be a caregiver, someone to lighten the load, or just someone to keep company. Maybe you are the sufferer. Then rejoice that you have a Christian friend who will walk beside you. Both sufferer and friend can grow in God's grace and sense the presence and blessing of Christ joining them in unique and intimate ways. Words fail to describe the breath of Christ that breathes His presence on you.

> "The Lord sees your sufferings with an eye of pity and
> also is able to achieve some good through them."
> —Isaac Penington[14]

Jesus' life and ministry remind us that living a godly life on this earth does not guarantee that everything will go in our favor. We so want to believe that it should. We want to think that those who drive a new car, wear new clothes, or win an award at work have God's favor. But we must never make that connection. Maybe those benefits reflect God blessing; maybe they do not. The fact that we didn't get a new car or win an award says nothing of God's disfavor either. Hardships will come our way just as they came to Jesus. We must learn to live in victory over them even as He did.

Faithful service to God and blessings from His hand do not exempt us from human suffering. Jesus was God's Son who did God's work, and He suffered more than any of us. We must be willing to join Him in suffering. We can rest assured that in those dark nights of the soul, whether ours or our friends', that Christ will be right by us comforting, aiding, and resourcing us for the days ahead. We are never forsaken! Christ is with us, and so is our friend.

Day 19

Remember: Life will bring suffering; you can face it with Christ on one side and your friend on the other.

My God, my God, why have you forsaken me? (Matt. 27:46).

Help us to help each other, Lord;

Each other's cross to bear.

Let each his friendly aid afford

And feel his brother's care . . .

Help us to build each other up,

Our little stock improve;

Increase our faith, confirm our hope,

And perfect us in love.

—Charles Wesley (1707-88)[15]

ENCOUNTERING CHRIST IN
MY FRIENDSHIPS

rendezvous

Day 20

FRIENDS

These are the twelve he appointed: Simon (to whom he gave the name Peter); James son of Zebedee and his brother John (to them he gave the name Boanerges, which means Sons of Thunder); Andrew, Philip, Bartholomew, Matthew, Thomas, James son of Alphaeus, Thaddaeus, Simon the Zealot and Judas Iscariot, who betrayed him (Mark 3:16-19).

Have you ever noticed how many popular television shows are about a group of friends going through life together? Sometimes they live in the same apartment complex. Sometimes they work at the same hospital or office building. Sometimes they attend the same school or are drawn together by age. The situations and settings of the television programs may differ, but the programs have one thing in common—group life.

Contemporary society creates many barriers that can drive people into silos of loneliness and alienation. Impersonal work cubicles, automated phone systems, and cyberspace often leave a person feeling like a disconnected soul floating in a boat lost at sea.

Planes, trains, and automobiles take us farther and faster than our grandparents ever dreamed possible. Satellite radio and television connect us continuously to our world. High-speed Internet and cell phones give us instant global communication. Yet in the midst of the most connected and mobile society in history, people complain that they are lonely and disconnected. That explains the renewed interest in television programs that spotlight group identity. By watching this kind of show, viewers feel somehow connected to the lives of the television characters and their group. Unfortunately, when the show ends, viewers go back to their lonely, disconnected lives. That may be why many people find great value in joining a group. They need to belong, fit in, contribute, and be needed.

It is no surprise that group identity provides many benefits. Christians have always valued group membership. Jesus showed us the importance of belonging to a group when He gathered 12 men around Him at the beginning of His public ministry. Our Scripture reading for today recounts that and names these individuals. The Twelve took nearly every step Jesus took throughout His earthly ministry; they heard nearly every word He spoke; they watched nearly every act He performed. The men in this close-knit group felt Jesus' heartbeat for needy humanity and found themselves challenged to live as He lived.

Jesus did not change His pattern of living when He came to earth to live with us in community. As the second member of the Trinity, He had lived a communal life from eternity past with His Father and the Holy Spirit. He will continue to live that way for eternity future with His Father, the Holy Spirit, and all of His followers. That's the good news of the gospel: we will join the Trinity someday for an eternity of sharing life together.

As we read the New Testament and begin to develop a picture of the Early Church, we realize that early Christians thought of themselves not as individual followers of Jesus Christ; rather they most often identified themselves as members of a group. Just like the Early Church, such a group identity tracks its way clearly throughout every generation of church history. Wherever followers of Jesus Christ go, they always band together in groups.

*Early Christians . . . most often identified themselves
as members of a group.*

Think for a minute of the possibilities for group identity in your Christian life. Perhaps you belong to a Sunday School class or an adult Bible study fellowship. Maybe you and your mate participate in a Bible study group with other couples your age. Men sometimes join men's Bible study groups while women gather together to study the Word from a woman's perspective. Athletes often share their Christian lives together. We even have a group of motorcycle enthusiasts at our church who meet weekly to ride their motorcycles and share their Christian walk. Possibilities for group participation abound within the Christian community!

This week we are going to continue our examination of exercises and practices of Christian living. We will see how we perform them as members of a small group. Long-term spiritual growth seldom occurs in isolation. Christ most often grows and develops His followers as they participate in groups. His Spirit lives in and works with our spirits individually. However, the friends in our small group encourage us, listen to us, hold us accountable, pray with us, correct us, are honest with us, tell us the truth about ourselves, pray for us, support us, stand by us, and sometimes carry us. They make themselves available to us 24/7. They accept and love us unconditionally for who we currently are and what Christ is transforming us to become. They live life together with us and call attention to Christ's work within each of us and within the group itself.

As members of the Christian community, we have the tremendous privilege of joining other Christians in small-group settings. Jesus established group identity as the norm for His followers while He walked this earth; He still blesses the benefits of small groups to this very day. We're all busy. We may even feel we can make it through life all by ourselves. But we really can't. We need the input and benefits that come to us through small-group interaction.

Take a minute and think about your current situation. Have you already committed yourself to a Sunday School class, small-group Bible study, or other Christian small group? If so, great! You're ready to move on to our exploration of this week's insights on Christian growth in a group setting.

If you have not committed yourself to a small group, decide where you might fit in and commit to joining. If you are struggling over where to plug in, talk to your pastor. Ask for help in finding a small group that will work best for you. Then read the material for this week with that group in mind. Promise yourself that before the week ends, you will take steps to become part of a small group. You'll be glad you did; your spiritual growth and development require it.

Day 20

Remember: Jesus usually grows and develops His followers in groups. *These are the twelve he appointed* (Mark 3:16).

Day 21

YOU REALLY BELONG

*Immediately Jesus made the disciples get into the boat and go on ahead of him
to the other side, while he dismissed the crowd. After he had dismissed them,
he went up on a mountainside by himself to pray. When evening came,
he was there alone, but the boat was already a considerable distance from land,
buffeted by the waves because the wind was against it* (Matt. 14:22-24).

Growing up on a farm gave me many opportunities to nurture my vivid imagination. My brothers and I used our imaginations to turn a simple farm shed or homemade tree house into a fort or headquarters for international spies. After we built our fortress, we would create rules and post a No Girls Allowed sign at the entrance. Since we lived on a farm at the end of a dirt road and didn't have any close neighbors, the sign only applied to one girl—our sister! Yes, we discriminated against her, but we also found ways to include her in some of our games and fantasies—after all, she was our sister. Once established, our fortress was where we played for hours, ate meals, and sometimes slept on warm nights. It was a great time to be together.

Those childhood memories illustrate the value of being part of a group. We four Moores grew up with each other, eating, playing, exploring, fighting, and doing just about everything else siblings do. Life happened to us as a family. We saw each other at our best and at our worst. We seldom put our best foot forward to impress one another—unless we wanted someone to do something for us! We accepted and supported each other. Our commitment to one another ran heart deep.

That was the way Jesus' disciples lived life together with their Master. They went through good and bad days together. They walked with Jesus through the easy times and the hard ones. Today's Scripture reading finds the disciples in trouble at sea, caught in the middle of a storm. They had just witnessed one of Jesus' greatest miracles: the feeding of 5,000 men and their families. Within hours the circumstances of life changed quickly, bringing peril. In the midst of their peril, Jesus performed another great miracle. He walked on the lake to assist them and invited Peter to walk with Him. Jesus' life with His disciples reminds us of the many spiritual benefits we enjoy together with members of our small group.

Let's look at a few spiritual practices we have already considered. This time, let's see how they look through the lens of a group. Again, the group might be a Sunday School class, Bible study fellowship, or accountability group.

Prayer. Prayer takes on a different dynamic when we pray with a group of Christians. Both personal prayer and prayer with an accountability partner are important for our spiritual lives. Yet God can work in and through us as members of a small group in entirely different ways.

For more than three decades I have taught a Sunday School class. We share prayer requests and answers in class, and we e-mail each other weekly. God regularly works through our prayers, sometimes performing health-related miracles that mystify even the doctors. I am confident that when our Sunday School class prays, positive things happen.

So when you have a special need, ask your small group to pray with you about it.

Bible study. Christians get together in small groups for a variety of reasons, as we discussed yesterday. Most of the time, however, they study the Bible. We must maintain our personal study of God's Word, as we discussed on Day 8. It's also helpful to share biblical insights with a trusted friend, as we discussed on Day 14. But we may learn some of the most important things in the Word when we study it with a group of friends. God has a way of speaking His truth through group members as they study passages of Scripture together. Each week I am amazed at what I learn through my friends as we study the

Word together. They share insights I never would have thought of on my own. They help me see beyond my limited point of view.

So open your Bible with your Bible study partners and let God instruct you through them.

Thinking. Group Bible study often leads to shared thinking about the meaning of a passage of Scripture or a doctrine. The insights my friends contribute lead to further discussions. Sometimes we talk about how to apply what we studied, what the pastor preached Sunday, or what a coworker said about faith. Sometimes our Bible study group gets so involved in the discussion that we continue it into the next week. Another person's viewpoint can put a totally different color on a thought for us. That's what I enjoy most about thinking together as Christians; my understanding is enriched and expanded by the contribution of others.

So let your Christian group help you think about your faith or Bible reading in new and interesting ways.

Examination. We have already considered personal examination and examination with a trusted friend. Now let's look at how this practice works in a small group. Most Bible study groups hold members accountable for their attendance and Bible reading. Some take the further step of having group members ask each other questions about their spiritual journey. John Wesley developed an entire system for nurturing believers using spiritual examination within a group. For this practice to be effective, group members must

- Be committed to the group for an extended period of time
- Trust one another
- Submit to one another
- Be open and honest with each other
- Maintain confidentiality with what members share

As with the practice of examination by an accountability partner, examination in a small group fosters our spiritual diligence in daily living. Weekly reports have a way of doing that!

So think about holding yourself accountable to your group for your walk with Christ.

Service/ministry. We have discussed doing acts of service and ministry as individuals and with a trusted friend. Serving or ministering alone or with another person is important. But we need the added spiritual dimension of serving or ministering as a group. Sunday School classes or Bible study groups often have service projects throughout the year. My Sunday School class does this very thing. Class members will get together at an appointed time and help needy people in the name of Jesus. Sometimes these needy people attend our church, but usually they are strangers in special need.

Groups from our church get together several times a year and tackle service projects in our community, in our state, and halfway around the world. A bond of fellowship develops among the people doing these projects that can be found nowhere else. We magnify our witness for Christ when the world sees our faith in action as we make life better for others.

So join with your group, roll up your sleeves, and do a service or ministry project.

These five practices only scratch the surface of the many ways we can grow spiritually through a group. They serve as reminders that Christ meets with us in new ways, even in the exercises we have already discussed in this book, when we do them with a group of friends. We really belong in a group!

Day 21

Remember: Christ meets you in new ways when you participate in a Christian group.

Immediately Jesus made the disciples get into the boat and go on ahead of him to the other side, while he dismissed the crowd (Matt. 14:22).

Day 22

ALL THE MORE TO SEE YOU WITH

Then he said to them all: "If anyone would come after me, he must deny himself and take up his cross daily and follow me. For whoever wants to save his life will lose it, but whoever loses his life for me will save it" (Luke 9:23-24).

One of the world's innovators of the global positioning system (GPS) has its headquarters and production plant a couple of blocks from our home. Many of our university students work there after they graduate. Supplying guidance systems for large commercial airliners, small private planes, semitrailer trucks, recreational vehicles, passenger cars, and even bikers and hikers has exploded into a big business in recent years. What's the premise of this new industry? People need directions.

We sometimes hate to admit it, but we all need directions from time to time. Whether we're trying to locate a business across town or find our way on vacation, getting someone's help with directions can be crucial to finding our way. What's true for road trips is true for the spiritual life as well. The Spirit of God sometimes instructs us deep within our heart and mind when we listen for His voice. He sometimes instructs us through an accountability partner. Today we want to explore the way God's Spirit instructs us through members of our small group.

Nearly everyone has sat in a circle of friends and heard advice on how to handle a particular problem. Some of the comments have merit; others are worthless. In the end, we may have a variety of options from which to choose. But that's not what we're talking about today. We're lifting our sights higher than just seeking a variety of personal opinions.

In our Scripture reading for today, Jesus sat and talked with His disciples about various topics. He first asked them who people thought He was (vv. 18-20). He then predicted His crucifixion (vv. 21-22). After that, Jesus gave His disciples spiritual direction on what it meant to be His follower. He contradicted the way people usually approached life; He called His disciples to deny themselves, live humbly, and follow His example.

The disciples did not simply sit in a circle and pool their opinions. They heard spiritual direction from One who knew the heart of God. Pooled opinions have some value. They offer us options and help us think in different ways. But they do not necessarily carry the weight of divine authority or the voice of God. Jesus' spiritual direction to His disciples had both divine authority and the voice of God.

Although Jesus has returned to His Father's side, He still provides spiritual direction to His disciples. Sometimes He directs us through the Bible. Sometimes we hear His voice through the ministry of His Spirit to our spirit. Sometimes—as we are seeing today—He speaks to us through members of our small group.

Although Jesus has returned to His Father's side,
He still provides spiritual direction to His disciples.

When functioning as spiritual directors, group members assist us in
- Discerning the work of God in our lives
- Listening for God's voice
- Recognizing the presence of God in our current situation
- Seeing our blind spots
- Living a life true to God's call

The details on our daily to-do list can so occupy us that we miss the big spiritual picture of our lives. One day becomes a week; weeks flow into years. Over time we lose touch with God's map for our spiritual journey. Group members assist us by giving us another set of eyes to see what God might be doing, or trying to do, in us. They give us another set of ears to hear both the loud and quiet ways God might be speaking to us.

> "We speak to one another on the basis of the help we both need. We admonish one another to go the way that Christ bids us to go. We warn one another against the disobedience that is our common destruction. We are gentle and we are severe with one another, for we know both God's kindness and God's severity."
> —Dietrich Bonhoeffer (1906-45)[16]

Spiritual direction from our group comes not from the pooled opinions of group members but from the Spirit of God as members attune themselves to the spiritual dimension of our lives. After all, true spiritual direction comes only from God's Spirit. God works through group members as they give themselves to all of the spiritual exercises we discussed on Days 6 to 12. Those exercises include quiet conversations, quiet listening, quiet reading, quiet thinking, quiet writing, quiet simplicity, and quiet examination. Group members perform these exercises and experience spiritual growth and development. This growth and development leads to spiritual maturity.

Spiritual maturity never implies perfection of performance, the lack of idiosyncrasies, or no further need for growth. All Christians remain works in progress. We all fall short of flawless performance. We all have idiosyncrasies. We all can grow in one way or another for as long as we live, both on this earth and in heaven. Yet in spite of our imperfections, God chooses to speak through us to offer spiritual instruction and direction to fellow travelers on the Christian way. If God can speak through a burning bush (Exod. 3:2) and a donkey (Num. 22:28), He can speak through fellow believers!

Small groups offer spiritual direction to group members in different ways. Some groups regularly give each member a chance to share problems or issues requiring spiritual direction. Other group members then share spiritual insights to address each problem or issue. Some groups make spiritual direction an occasional feature of their meetings. They offer spiritual direction only when group members speak up with a particular spiritual need.

The timing for spiritual direction also varies. It can be offered during the meeting or later in the week after group members have had time to pray about and reflect on an issue. They may communicate in person, on the phone, or through e-mail. The structure or timing for offering spiritual direction is not nearly as important as having group members participate with us in hearing and responding to the voice of God in our lives.

In the children's fable *Little Red Riding Hood,* the little girl with the red hood asked the imposter in her grandmother's bed why she had such big eyes. "All the more to see you with" was the imposter's reply. Our eyes are never big enough to see all that God wants to do in us. That's why we need the bigger eyes of our small group to offer us spiritual direction so we can better see God's bigger picture.

Open yourself this week to the spiritual direction of your group. Let God instruct you in new ways as He speaks to you through group members. You'll be amazed at how God can communicate to you through your trusted friends. In doing this you will once again encounter Christ in a unique way.

Day 22

Remember: God often offers spiritual direction for your life through your small group. Listen carefully!

For whoever wants to save his life will lose it,
but whoever loses his life for me will save it (Luke 9:24).

Day 23

A MOUNTAINTOP EXPERIENCE

About eight days after Jesus said this, he took Peter, John and James with him and went up onto a mountain to pray. As he was praying, the appearance of his face changed, and his clothes became as bright as a flash of lightning (Luke 9:28-29).

On Day 21 I told you about the fortress my siblings and I made while growing up on the farm. Sometimes we imagined our fortress was a church building and we were the ones conducting the worship. Since no other children lived near us, we boosted our attendance by inviting all of our pets. We brought dogs, cats, ducks, geese, and chickens to the fort. We made the cows observe through the windows. My sister led the singing, and I preached the sermon. I guess that was my first experience with small-group worship.

In our Scripture reading for today we see Jesus engaged with three of His disciples and two guests in small-group worship. The account continues through verse 36. Read the entire passage for the whole story. The group had quite an amazing time of worship. The participants were especially interesting. They included Jesus, Peter, James, John, Moses, and Elijah. The last two were very special guests, since they had been in heaven for several hundred years.

On Days 6 to 12 we discussed several ways to encounter God individually. We talked about spending time with God in prayer, meditation, Bible reading, reflection, writing, and examination. Each of these activities is a way to worship God privately. Many times we limit our definition of *worship* to what an entire congregation of Christians does on a Sunday morning or at some other set time together. Worship certainly should occur at those times, and we will look closer at congregational worship next week. But now we need to expand our understanding of worship to look at how we worship God in a small group.

We usually think of the elements of worship as singing, praying, Scripture reading, special music, and a sermon. These elements certainly belong in many worship settings. But by themselves these activities do not capture the essence of worship. True worship is not a matter of a certain style of music, a certain set of musical instruments, a certain type of prayer, or any certain activity. Rather, true worship flows from

- Loving God and valuing Him more than all else in life
- Seeking God's kingdom first
- Obeying God and glorifying Him with our lives
- Praising, adoring, and delighting in God
- Thinking about the mystery and wonder of God
- Sitting silently in the presence of God
- Focusing on God and seeking to know Him better

Look at the action verbs in the list above. Each verb calls us to do a specific thing in our relationship with God. Faith involves believing and trusting God with our heart and mind. Worship involves putting that belief and trust into action so our faith can come to life.

Many of the items listed above can and should take place at some point in Christian small-group meetings. Look back at the small-group worship event in Luke 9. Notice how many of these elements occurred.

Verses 28-36 do not mention singing or preaching. But they do stress communing with the Father. The group worshiped the Father as they prayed and rehearsed the value Jesus placed on doing the Father's will, even to the point of His death. Notice what happened at the end of the worship session. The Father visited the group and spoke to them. That is the highest honor God gives any worship session!

Think about the small group you attend and answer the following questions about it.

1. Which of the elements of worship listed above are already present in your group meetings?
2. In what activities do you include these elements?
3. Which of the elements could you add to make your time together more meaningful and worshipful?
4. How might you effectively accomplish this?

Jesus and His disciples certainly had a mountaintop experience in Luke 9. What made it so memorable? We already know it was not the activities they did together. So what was it? Their time together was memorable because the Father joined them. They did not coax the Father to join them. They simply worshiped Him, and He came. Every time you meet with your small group, remember the words of Jesus, "For where two or three come together in my name, there am I with them" (Matt. 18:20).

Be sure your small-group meetings always include elements of worship. As you worship together, be ready to encounter Christ; He promised to be there.

Day 23

Remember: Time together in a small group with other Christian believers can always be a great time for worship.

About eight days after Jesus said this, he took Peter, John and James with him and went up onto a mountain to pray (Luke 9:28).

Day 24

SHALL WE GATHER AT THE PARTY

On the third day a wedding took place at Cana in Galilee. Jesus' mother was there, and Jesus and his disciples had also been invited to the wedding (John 2:1-2).

Our Sunday School class loves to be together. They can think of more ways than anyone else to get together and eat! They celebrate every religious and national holiday they know. I think they'd get together to celebrate Independence Day in Finland if they knew the date! Every social gathering involves food. Sometimes we have a potluck dinner at church. Sometimes class members cook all of the food, and we eat in homes. Sometimes we go to a restaurant. Food is not needed for fellowship, but it sure is a nice bonus!

What draws us together? Is it the food? Is it the party atmosphere? No, we love to get together because we enjoy Christian fellowship. Such fellowship is a vital part of Christian life. So often we think of seeing Jesus or growing spiritually only through prayer, Bible reading, meditation, thinking, journaling, examination, worship, and the many other spiritual practices. These practices may appear more pious than Christian fellowship, but they are certainly not more important. Fellowship plays a vital role in spiritual growth.

In our Scripture reading for today, Jesus and His disciples attended a wedding. We are not looking at this passage because it tells about the incredible miracle Jesus performed—the first miracle of His public ministry. We are looking at this passage because it reminds us that Jesus spent a great deal of time with His disciples in social settings. They ate and drank together frequently. In fact, the last event Jesus shared with His disciples before His crucifixion was a meal (Luke

22:7-38). He even shared a meal with His disciples following His resurrection (John 21:10-14). These examples, among others, remind us that Jesus made an important place for Christian fellowship.

What happens when we fellowship together with our small group? First, we see the Christian life lived out through a shared meal with our friends. Such settings provide a great way to introduce new Christians to the enjoyment of sharing in the lives of other Christians. Second, we encourage each other as we talk and laugh together. So much of life involves work, responsibility, concentration, and stress. Christian fellowship allows us to unwind and be ourselves with one another in a safe setting.

Third, this type of fellowship provides accountability. Group members know whether or not we are present. If they sense we are falling away from the group, they can intervene to draw us back to the center of the fellowship and keep us faithful. Few believers fall away from Christ and His Church without first drifting away from accountability to their immediate group.

Fourth, times of fellowship create an atmosphere for group members to open up and share their burdens. Such sharing creates an opportunity for members to support one another. Finally, we should remember that eating together is one of the most endearing social events. Shared meals bring people together in inviting ways. When Christians fellowship together, especially around a table of food, they strengthen their bonds with one another.

I know how important Christian fellowship can be to the life of small-group members because I grew up watching it in action. I cannot remember a single Sunday afternoon during my childhood that our family did not eat lunch and spend the afternoon in another Christian family's home or that we did not bring another family home with us for lunch. The children played together while the parents talked about life, faith, and the Christian journey. I look back on those memories fondly because those small-group social settings helped me see Christianity as more than a religion. In a very real sense I came to see it as a shared life of vital interactions with other believers.

Think about your social activities for the last week or the last month. What percentage of them involved other Christian believers? We must maintain our primary social identity with other Christians. Certainly, we should interact with workmates as well as non-Christian family members, friends, and neighbors. However, these interactions should not constitute our primary social identity. We need to reserve valuable time to be with fellow believers.

Christian fellowship offers something special not found in the world's social gatherings. The world can provide a meeting place, food, music, and drink. But it cannot provide the unique camaraderie that Christians feel when they meet together. That special bond cannot be duplicated!

So meet together often with your Christian friends. As you do, look for ways that Christ meets with you. Remember the words we quoted yesterday from Jesus: "For where two or three come together in my name, there am I with them" (Matt. 18:20). His presence is not limited to Bible studies or worship services; He also is with Christians when they come together for fellowship. Don't be surprised after you return home from a Christian party or small-group potluck dinner if you sense that you've just been in the presence of Jesus. You probably have!

Day 24

Remember: Christian fellowship provides us with a great opportunity to enjoy life with other Christians and sense the Lord's presence at the same time.

On the third day a wedding took place at Cana in Galilee. Jesus' mother was there, and Jesus and his disciples had also been invited to the wedding (John 2:1-2).

Day 25

WITH OPEN ARMS

"Love the Lord your God with all your heart and with all your soul and with all your mind and with all your strength." The second is this: "Love your neighbor as yourself." There is no commandment greater than these (Mark 12:30-31).

On Day 11 I mentioned that for 20 years Sue and I took a group of our university students to other countries over spring break to build church buildings or homes and to minister to needy people. On every trip and in every country, the local residents showed their appreciation by hosting us for a special meal. Sometimes the food looked familiar. But usually it did not resemble anything we had ever seen or eaten before. On those occasions, we instructed our students (and ourselves) not to ask too many questions about the food or how they prepared it. We all just took a deep breath and ate it!

Those occasions always rehearsed for us the cardinal rule of hospitality. That is, we do not gather to consume exquisitely prepared food or marvel at the beauty of the host home. Rather, good hospitality gives guests the opportunity to share the love of God in Jesus' name. I have been the recipient of hospitality at thousands of meals in more homes than I can recount. Some of those homes topped the list of desirable real estate. Others were meager by any standard. I can no longer recall the food we ate together, but I will never forget the fellowship we always enjoyed. Christian fellowship has an unforgettable quality. Why? The presence of Christ communes with the hearts of His followers when they get together.

In our Scripture reading for today, Jesus rehearsed the two most important commandments from the Old Testament law. We are looking at the second one today because it says something important about hospitality. But we must practice the first commandment, love God, before we can practice the second. We love Him and others because He first loved us. The love God gives us motivates us to open our lives and our homes to others in hospitable ways. We give to others because He has given to us. He set the example by loving us. We follow that example and pass the blessing along.

Hospitality is more than just eating a meal together, even though that happens frequently. Hospitality also includes opening our home to give someone a place to stay. We show hospitality when we give someone a ride in our car. We may even loan or give someone a car. We might share any of our resources with another person as well.

Attention is not on the act of hospitality itself but always the safe environment it creates when we welcome a friend, stranger, or an enemy in Jesus' name. We offer this safe environment regardless of how people have treated us in the past or how we think they might treat us in the future. We act as conduits of God's love and thus can freely offer what we have so freely received.

> "Lose no opportunity of doing good in any kind.
> Be zealous of good works; willingly omit no work,
> either of piety or mercy. Do all the good you possibly
> can, to the bodies and souls of men."
> —John Wesley[17]

Our world can be impersonal. People easily get lost along the sidelines. In order to fit in, they often feel compelled to make a good impression on others or create a positive image about themselves. When we give people the free space of a safe, hospitable environment, they feel released from having to make a good impression or cast a positive image. The person who receives our Christian hospitality can sit back, relax, and let down all defenses.

Hospitality actually comes from the Latin word *hospitalitas,* which means "friendliness to guests." It shares the same root with the word *hospital,* which is a "house for healing." Together these meanings merge into a beautiful image! Christian hospitality provides a welcoming place for people to come and heal.

> *Almost limitless human need creates a variety of ways for us to reach out to others in hospitality.*

Our reason for offering hospitality should always be to love people rather than impress them. We want to set them at ease rather than create an obligation to respond in a certain way or repay us for our efforts. In fact, hospitality often yields the greatest benefits when offered to those who do not have the ability to repay us. We may even find ways to show hospitality anonymously. In those cases, recipients of our hospitality may never know our name. That's all right; we give in Jesus' name and for His glory, not our own.

The small-group setting lends itself well to practicing hospitality. Often the social gatherings of my Sunday School class, which I referenced yesterday, become opportunities for class members to offer hospitality. On those occasions, we reach out to visitors at our church, unchurched friends and neighbors, and anyone else who might enjoy such a gathering. At other times Sunday School class members reach out to others by opening their homes to those going through hard times. Class members work together to minister to the whole person by providing clothes, cosmetics, or other needs for these people.

Almost limitless human need creates a variety of ways for us to reach out to others in hospitality. Think of ways you can take the concepts we have discussed today and apply them to your particular situation in life and with your small group. What do you have to offer others? A home or apartment, a car, money, a listening ear, your time? Who can be the recipients of your hospitality? Family members, close friends, neighbors, visitors to your group, strangers, enemies? When can you make your offer of hospitality to others? Soon, sometime in the future, never?

Only you can answer these questions. They require you to step out of your comfort zone and offer yourself and your resources in Jesus' name. It requires an element of confidence and security on your part. The good news is it does not have to be your confidence and security. You can draw these and everything else you need to practice hospitality from Christ.

Reaching out to others in hospitality offers us another avenue to sense the presence of Christ as we minister in His name.

Day 25

Remember: Loving others as ourselves includes reaching out to them in Christian hospitality.

The second is this: "Love your neighbor as yourself." There is no commandment greater than these (Mark 12:31).

Day 26

BEAR ONE ANOTHER'S BURDENS

When Jesus saw her weeping, and the Jews who had come along with her also weeping, he was deeply moved in spirit and troubled. "Where have you laid him?" he asked. "Come and see, Lord," they replied. Jesus wept (John 11:33-35).

On Day 19 I briefly related the story of Kevin and Janell. Let me expand the account today. Their story provides a beautiful example of a small group suffering together. Sometimes we suffer alone in silence. Things improve when we have a friend or family member bearing the burden of suffering with us. What's even better is when our small group shares in our suffering.

Kevin received the news of his brain tumor while living in Nashville. Since Janell worked full time, she could not always drive him to his doctor's appointments or radiation treatments following the diagnosis. Members of their Sunday School class stepped in and took turns driving Kevin to his medical appointments and treatments. Janell says she never would have made it through those difficult days without the help of faithful friends from their small group. They suffered together with this precious couple and lightened their load in practical ways.

Five years later when the tumors reappeared on Kevin's brain X-rays, they lived in our area. This time medical intervention included several surgeries and many follow-up treatments. Again, Sunday School class members stepped in to assist with trips to the doctor, meals, work around the house, and other means of support. Yesterday we considered the spiritual practice of hospitality. Kevin and Janell received the benefits of hospitality as class members carried the burden of suffering with them in a whole host of daily tasks.

In our Scripture reading for today, Jesus joined a small group who suffered with Mary and Martha at the death of their brother Lazarus. You will want to read the entire story again in verses 1-44. Notice how Jesus, His disciples, and friends from the community came to comfort the two sisters as they grieved the loss of their brother. Jesus expressed the emotion of the entire group when He was deeply moved in spirit and troubled. The shortest verse in the Bible contains one of the most powerful messages of the Bible: "Jesus wept" (v. 35). Only two words, but oh what a message! The great God of the universe cared so deeply for His two friends who had lost their brother that He broke down and cried with them. What a beautiful picture of God suffering with our hurts!

We need not re-create all of the discussion presented on Day 19 regarding suffering with a friend or accountability partner. To quickly summarize, we stated that

- Everyone on earth suffers at one time or another in this life.
- Suffering can be a good disciple-making tool.
- Suffering can help prepare our souls for eternity.
- Suffering comes our way through an almost endless variety of sources.
- The load of suffering can be lightened when shared with others.

God gives us friends to share our times of suffering.

That last point draws our attention to today's important truth: God gives us friends to share our times of suffering. I've watched it happen for more than 35 years as a member of a small group of Christian believers, usually a Sunday School class. As I teach my class the weekly Bible lesson, I know the Bible's message works in the trenches because I've watched it lived out in the life of our group. A very significant part of that group life has included times of shared suffering, bearing one another's burdens.

Kevin and Janell's story involved physical suffering. Other class members have gone through deep emotional and relational suffering: a spouse was unfaithful, a son disowned his parents, and a daughter was lost in a tragic automobile accident. Class members have suffered financial reversals too: the loss of a job, an unexpected lawsuit, and the unplanned responsibility of raising grandchildren. They have also struggled through the sandwich years—caring for elderly parents while helping their children plan marriages and start families.

The stories all fall into unique categories, but each is a type of suffering. Such suffering can drive people to alcohol, drug abuse, or depression. Christian believers have something better—each other. Like Jesus, they feel the pain of their friends and they weep. Then they share the load their friends are bearing.

Christian believers have something better—each other!

Think about members of your small group and the types of suffering they face. How have you helped them? How have they helped you? How could you all do a better job of supporting each other?

You might be surprised to learn that supporting each other through suffering is another way to encounter Jesus. Receiving the blessing of His presence is not the sole reason we bear the burdens of others. Yet He often comes to us as we share in the hurt and heartache of our friends.

So bear one another's burdens in your small group and watch Jesus make himself known to you.

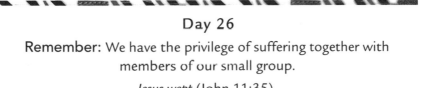

Day 26
Remember: We have the privilege of suffering together with members of our small group.
Jesus wept (John 11:35).

"Christianity means community through Jesus Christ and in Jesus Christ. No Christian community is more or less than this. Whether it be a brief, single encounter or the daily fellowship of years, Christian community is only this. We belong to one another only through and in Jesus Christ."

—Dietrich Bonhoeffer[18]

ENCOUNTERING CHRIST IN
MY FAITH COMMUNITY

rendezvous

Day 27

THE BODY OF CHRIST

He went to Nazareth, where he had been brought up, and on the Sabbath day he went into the synagogue, as was his custom (Luke 4:16).

Like a lot of young boys, I had dreams of becoming a cowboy when I grew up. What a way of life! Live out on the range alone. Eat beans from a can. Drink coffee out of a tin cup. Ride your horse all day, and sleep on the ground at night. Who could ask for anything more?

So with a six-shooter (a cap gun of course) strapped to my six-year-old waist, and a cowboy hat on my head, I practiced being a cowboy. The only difference between me and most little guys these days is that we lived on a farm with real cows, horses, and herding dogs. When I grew up, I realized that the solitary life of the cowboy was not everything I'd imagined it to be. I needed other people to make my life complete. What's true of daily life holds true as well in the Christian faith.

I'm amazed at the number of Christians in the 21st century who only want a Jesus-and-me religion. They're disillusioned with organized religion or do not see themselves fitting into the larger Christian community. Many of them have said to me, "I love Jesus, but I don't want anything to do with the organized Christian Church." That's unfortunate because Jesus never taught a solitary religion like we're seeing practiced these days.

Our verse of Scripture for today speaks volumes about the priorities and practices of Jesus' religious life. The verse simply tells us that on the weekly day of worship Jesus went to church "as was his custom" (v. 16). Worship attendance for Jesus was more than a twice-a-year event or something done on occasion. His common practice brought Him to the house of God weekly, giving us an example to follow.

129

Jesus' custom of going to church weekly reminds us of the rich heritage of the Hebrew faith recorded in the Old Testament. Jesus followed carefully the customs and practices of this heritage. He knew every detail of the Old Testament and followed its teachings carefully, committing much of it to memory. Jesus knew that the Father originally directed all of the admonitions and promises of the Old Testament to a faith community.

We in the New Testament age often apply these promises to our individual lives. We can do this as long as we remember they apply to us individually within the corporate community of faith. The New Testament understanding of salvation is about making an individual decision to ask Christ for forgiveness of personal sins and the acceptance of Christ as personal Savior. However, once a person decides to follow Christ, he or she must never attempt to live a Christian life in solitary confinement. The example of Jesus clearly points to our identity in the corporate community.

This week we will look at ways we encounter Christ in our faith community. Some of the spiritual practices of community life will flow from ideas we have already discussed. Others will be brand-new. In both cases, Christ can intersect our lives through a faith community in ways that can happen nowhere else. If we cut ourselves off from our faith community, we limit Christ's work in us. Just as we need time alone, time with an accountability partner, and time in a small group for spiritual growth, we also need time with an entire community of faith.

When we join the Christian community, we enter a dimension of spiritual life that connects us to others in ways that encourage growth in Christ. Community life creates space for us to enjoy relationships that bring Christ to life within the community. This connection to one another and Christ allows Him to reveal himself to us in special ways.

Without even realizing it, a spirit of independence can work against our spiritual growth. We may be tempted to assume with

pride a rugged-individualist attitude—an attitude of not needing anyone else on our spiritual journey. Such an attitude usually brags about being strong enough to make the journey alone. This trick of Satan will assure our defeat. None of us possess all of the spiritual fortitude we need to make the journey of life alone. That's why God gives us a faith community.

A spirit of independence promotes isolation, self-absorption, and self-centeredness. Christ wants us to replace a spirit of independence with one of dependence upon one another and Him. Along with this we need a spirit of interdependence to bind us together in a web that will make us stronger together than any of us could be apart.

The Bible has more to say about all this than we can possibly consider this week. For starters, consider the image of the Body of Christ. Paul discussed this image in detail in 1 Cor. 12:12-27. He said we have been baptized by one Spirit into one body. He then talked about various parts of the human body and how they all work together. Feet, hands, ears, eyes, and nose all make their contribution to the greater good of the whole body. Each part needs the other. He concluded his discussion with this important reminder, "Now you are the body of Christ, and each one of you is a part of it" (v. 27).

So we really do need each other. Let's explore that idea this week and look for a few of the many ways Christ appears to us as we participate in our faith community.

Day 27

Remember: God forms Christian believers into the Body of Christ and works best through the whole group.

On the Sabbath day he went into the synagogue, as was his custom (Luke 4:16).

Day 28

ONLY IN THE GROUP

And he stood up to read. The scroll of the prophet Isaiah was handed to him. Unrolling it, he found the place where it is written: "The Spirit of the Lord is on me, because he has anointed me to preach good news to the poor. He has sent me to proclaim freedom for the prisoners and recovery of sight for the blind, to release the oppressed, to proclaim the year of the Lord's favor" (Luke 4:16b-19).

I grew up in a small New Testament church. I call it a New Testament church because it looked a great deal like the early days of the Church described in Acts 2:42-47. I did not know it at the time, but the biblical sermons, the fellowship of Christian believers in both worship and social settings, the breaking of bread both in Communion services and at potlucks, and the prayer life of the faith community helped shape me into the Christian I became in adulthood.

Our Scripture reading for today picks up where we left off yesterday. Jesus led His first worship service in His hometown church. If you read through verse 30, you will see that the event could have gone better! Always remember on occasions when you feel undervalued or misunderstood that you are in good company with Jesus. Our emphasis in this passage is not on the success or failure of Jesus' ministry in His home church but on the several worship activities that were taking place. Corporate worshipers in Jesus' day prayed, read Scripture, heard a sermon, and participated in many other practices just as we do.

Today, we want to look back over five spiritual practices we discussed earlier. This time we will see how they apply when the faith community comes together. Notice how the same activity brings the presence of the living Christ to us in a different way when we gather together with the whole Body of Believers.

Notice how the same activity brings the presence of the living Christ to us in a different way when we gather together with the whole Body of Believers.

Prayer. This is the fourth time we have considered the subject of prayer. We have talked about praying in private, praying with a trusted friend or mate, and praying in a small group. Now we want to see how prayer works differently as we pray with our whole faith community. Each setting holds an important place in our spiritual growth.

I cannot tell you why, but something special happens when we pray together with a congregation of believers. Sometimes we each pray silently; sometimes we all pray out loud; sometimes an individual leads in prayer. Sometimes we sit; sometimes we stand; sometimes we pray around the altars of the church. When we pray together, we pray for one another's needs and we pray for common concerns. Joining our hearts and minds together as a group reminds us of our place in a bigger picture. God renews our spiritual strength and courage as He encompasses us into this important group He calls His family.

So the next time you pray together with your whole faith community, remember the spiritual strength that comes from uniting with this army of saints.

Bible reading. A gathering of a faith community cannot be complete without reading the Bible corporately. Something special happens when we hear the Word of God together. Maybe that's because the Bible makes most of its promises to the family of God as a whole. Bible reading takes on a new dimension as we listen from the pew. Sometimes we hear the Word as a separate segment of the worship service; sometimes we hear it as a prelude to the sermon. Either way, the Spirit of God often speaks to us in fresh ways when we consider the biblical message as a word for the whole congregation. The reading reminds us again that we hear from God corporately.

So the next time you hear the Word together with your whole

faith community, remember His promises will sustain you because you belong to His family.

Thinking. Hearing the Bible, the words of a Christian song, the testimony of a saint of God, or a sermon while sitting with the family of God can set our minds to thinking in entirely different ways than if we heard these same words alone or in a small group. Perhaps we benefit from hearing the message aloud rather than reading it. Perhaps the benefit stems from hearing it with trusted Christian friends. Regardless of the reason, the fact remains: Christ may meet with you and set your mind to thinking exciting new thoughts as you gather with His saints. A woman once told me she was discouraged because her recent loss of eyesight had robbed her of the ability to do her work in ministry. But as she sat in a corporate worship service, the Lord set her mind to thinking about new avenues of ministry she could do as a blind woman.

So the next time you worship with God's family, don't be surprised if Christ fills your mind with brand-new thoughts.

Accountability. Sometimes we feel so accountable to everyone: family members, bosses, schoolteachers, or neighbors. Sometimes we wish we could just fade into the woodwork and be noticed by no one. You know as well as I do—that seldom happens. I don't suppose I've gone to a restaurant in our town in the last 20 years and not been recognized by friends.

Something like that happens when we attend church. People recognize us and take note of our presence. Over time that creates a pattern of accountability. People notice our absence. Hopefully they care enough about us to contact us and discover why we are missing. The accountability may not be as intimate as with our accountability partner, such as we discussed on Day 13. Nonetheless, the congregation holds us responsible as well. We have a unique role to play in the Body of Christ. No one else can replace us. Our absence leaves the Body without an important part.

So the next time you feel like fading into the woodwork, remember your accountability to the Body of Christ.

Fellowship. Acts 2:42 names fellowship as an important function of the Early Church. They enjoyed the spiritual fellowship of the Lord's Supper and the social fellowship of shared meals. Verse 46 seems to indicate that Early Church members ate together on a regular basis. Small-group fellowship plays an important role in spiritual growth, and so does fellowship within the faith community as a whole. All of the spiritual benefits of fellowship discussed on Day 24 apply to the large-group setting as well. Today we add in the idea that we are participating in the body life of a living organism. Yes, more than a social organization, the church is a living organism.

So the next time you attend an all-church social event, stand back for a minute and see the Body of Christ in action. Only in the gathered faith community will you see Jesus just like this! I began this reading by referring to my childhood church as a New Testament one. As I look again at verses 46-47, I see the effect of their activity together. The Bible says

- The group experienced gladness and sincerity of heart.
- They reached a focal point of praising God.
- Outsiders looked on them with favor.
- New people accepted Christ regularly and joined their fellowship.

Not a bad example for us today, is it?

Day 28

Remember: Christ often meets us in unique ways as we join together with the Body of Christ.

The Spirit of the Lord is on me, because he has anointed me to preach good news to the poor. He has sent me to proclaim freedom for the prisoners and recovery of sight for the blind, to release the oppressed, to proclaim the year of the Lord's favor (Luke 4:18-19).

Day 29

CELEBRATION TIME!

They brought it to Jesus, threw their cloaks on the colt and put Jesus on it. As he went along, people spread their cloaks on the road. When he came near the place where the road goes down the Mount of Olives, the whole crowd of disciples began joyfully to praise God in loud voices for all the miracles they had seen: "Blessed is the king who comes in the name of the Lord!" "Peace in heaven and glory in the highest!" (Luke 19:35-38).

Nature offers us some of the most beautiful sights in life—a glowing sunrise over the mountains, a shimmering sunset across the lake. They may not be heaven, but they're not far from it. All the beauty of nature, however, pales in comparison to the beauty of the people of God gathered together in His name worshiping Him with one heart and voice. It may not be heaven, but it's probably closer than anything else!

Our Scripture reading for today joins us with the Triumphal Entry of Jesus into Jerusalem for Passion Week. Excitement charged the air in anxious anticipation of God's work. Men threw their coats in the pathway of the coming Messiah. Women and children swung branches from palm trees in praise before Him. Worship of God rang to the highest heavens with songs of praise. When the Pharisees urged Jesus to gain control of the situation, Jesus observed, "If they keep quiet, the stones will cry out" (v. 40). What a time of celebration!

Celebration should characterize our times of corporate worship with the Body of Christ. We take pleasure in God as we glorify and praise Him for who He is and what He means to us. Worship offers us an opportunity to thank Him for His incredible plan of salvation along with His daily blessings to us. It also gives us a chance to look upward, beyond our difficulties, to the God whom we adore more than all else. It reminds us to place all our hope in Him. Worship gives us time to delight in the God of our salvation.

Look back over the account of the Triumphal Entry of Jesus. Now look back over the last paragraph of this reading. Pay special attention to words like *celebrate, take pleasure, glorify, praise, thanksgiving, look upward, hope,* and *delight*. Notice that everything we have talked about today refers to our gifts to God, not the benefits we receive in return. It always sounds strange to my ears when I hear people say, "I quit going to church because I just didn't get anything out of the experience." So what! Worship is not about us. It's not about getting; it's about giving. Worship is about giving to God all of our attention, praise, and glory.

Remember the list of essential elements we established for worship on Day 23? Review that list again.

- Loving God and valuing Him more than all else in life
- Seeking God's kingdom first
- Obeying God and glorifying Him with our lives
- Praising, adoring, and delighting in God
- Thinking about the mystery and wonder of God
- Sitting silently in the presence of God
- Focusing on God and seeking to know Him better

On Day 23 we applied this list to worship with a small group. Now look at the list as it relates to your worship with the entire Body of Christ. Our participation in corporate worship brings our faith to life in unique ways.

Believers gathered as a faith community have a variety of ways to worship God. This adds depth and breadth to our understanding of the many ways people can offer praise. We hear testimonies of God's work among all of His people, not just our small group. Small groups tend to be age- or interest-specific. An entire faith community is a cross section of all God's family. The testimonies of God's people in such a gathering give us a broader look at God's provisions and benefits.

We listen to the full range of parts and voices as the entire Body of

Christ sings songs of worship and praise to God. Solos, duets, and small ensembles have their place. But nothing replaces the full sound of all of the voices in God's house singing songs of worship with full volume. We listen as a whole Body to God's Word in the sermon. As the entire faith community sits in silence, the minister delivers the message God has for that particular occasion. This God-ordained event carries divine authority as the Holy Spirit applies the spoken Word to listening hearts.

Church parishioners across the land have engaged in lively discussions regarding the best worship elements and styles for the greatest spiritual effect. An almost infinite variety of elements and styles exist for today's worship experiences. Like seasoning on food, we all have our preferences. I do not like hot sauce on my food, but my dad pours gallons on everything he eats. It's all about personal preference. No instrument, beat, or music style carries more divine authority than another. None, in and of itself, brings a better blessing from God. We must assure that our discussions on corporate worship unite rather than divide our congregations.

As you approach corporate celebration time, keep the essential elements of worship in mind. Then praise God with your whole heart! You will encounter Christ as you offer your best to Him in the company of your faith community.

Day 29

Remember: Worship is not about you.
It's not about getting; it's about giving.

"Blessed is the king who comes in the name of the Lord!"
"Peace in heaven and glory in the highest!" (Luke 19:38).

Day 30

OUTWARD SIGNS

While they were eating, Jesus took bread, gave thanks and broke it, and gave it to his disciples, saying, "Take it; this is my body." Then he took the cup, gave thanks and offered it to them, and they all drank from it. "This is my blood of the covenant, which is poured out for many," he said to them (Mark 14:22-24).

My wife and I have many special memories of our son's childhood. One of our favorites happened during his preschool years. Every time we took Communion at church, I would whisper the meaning of the ritual to him each step of the way. Then I would serve him the elements. In time the Lord's Supper became his favorite part of corporate worship. Whenever we walked into the sanctuary and saw the Communion table spread, he would say, "Great. We get to have that special meal!" What a priceless priority for a little one. What a cherished memory.

Baptism and the Lord's Supper offer us two outward signs of the inward working of God's grace in our lives. These two symbols better express what transpires in our heart and spiritual life than words can ever convey. Jesus placed significance on both ceremonies during His earthly ministry and commanded us to do both.

Baptism and the Lord's Supper better express what transpires in our heart and spiritual life than words can ever convey.

Baptism remains one of the central symbols of the Christian faith. It symbolizes a number of spiritual truths. Here are a few of them:

- Baptism symbolizes new birth. It testifies to a radical spiritual transformation in us.

- Baptism symbolizes God washing our sins away, just as a bath washes dirt from our bodies.
- Baptism symbolizes the coming of the Holy Spirit into our lives. With the stain of sin washed away, our hearts become a clean place for the Spirit to live. Paul said in 1 Cor. 3:16 that we are God's temple and that His Spirit lives in us.
- Baptism symbolizes that God will remain faithful to His promise to save us. He saves us from a sinful life now and takes us to be with Him in eternity when we die.
- Baptism symbolizes entering into a contract with God and pledging ourselves to be faithful to the Christian faith. It replaces the Old Testament symbol of circumcision.
- Baptism symbolizes the completion of a spiritual transaction with God. Something happened both from God's perspective and from ours. It is an event in time, not a process throughout life, the same way we were dry one moment and wet the next in baptism. Sure, we will grow in the grace of God. But we have passed through the doorway and into the room of salvation.
- Baptism symbolizes a grave. We die and are buried with Christ as we are lowered into the water. As we come up, we are raised to new life in Him. Paul gives an extended explanation of this idea in Rom. 6:1-11. As he said in verse 4, "We were therefore buried with him through baptism into death in order that, just as Christ was raised from the dead through the glory of the Father, we too may live a new life."

We only observe some rituals of our faith once in a lifetime, as with baptism. We observe other rituals often, as with the Lord's Supper. We also call this ritual Communion or Eucharist. *Communion* means "fellowship" or "participation." We experience a special fellowship with the Lord when we take Communion. *Eucharist* means "giving thanks." Thus we enact our thankfulness for salvation. The phrase *Lord's Supper* reminds us of the evening of Christ's betrayal.

The Lord's Supper symbolizes several spiritual truths. Here are a few of them:

- The bread represents the body of Christ, the drink His blood. His body was broken and His blood spilled for our salvation. Blood symbolizes life, so the spilling of blood represents life being given. Thus the Lord's Supper memorializes Christ's death (1 Cor. 11:26).

- Christ's death completed the Old Testament sacrificial system. He became our Passover Lamb, sacrificed for our sins (5:7). Hebrews 9:11-28 gives a full presentation of this subject. Verse 14 especially paints this picture: "How much more, then, will the blood of Christ, who through the eternal Spirit offered himself unblemished to God, cleanse our consciences from acts that lead to death, so that we may serve the living God!" Christ's sacrifice far surpasses the requirements of the Old Testament sacrificial system because it gives us a clear conscience with God. Every participation in this special meal reaffirms that clear conscience.

- The Lord's Supper reminds us of God's promise to bring us together again someday to celebrate "the marriage supper of the Lamb" with Christ as an honored guest. This will happen at the end of time. During His last meal with His disciples, Jesus promised, "I tell you, I will not drink of this fruit of the vine from now on until that day when I drink it anew with you in my Father's kingdom" (Matt. 26:29). John saw a vision during God's revelation to him of that meal we will share together (Rev. 19:9). What a feast it will be, not because of the menu but because of Jesus' presence.

- We participate in this ritual as a testimony to our faith in Christ and a time of spiritual renewal. Eating and drinking remind us that our spirits receive spiritual strength from God the same way our bodies receive physical strength from eating food. At the same time, God uses this practice as a means of grace to strengthen us spiritually. For this reason some Christians take Communion every day or every week, though most receive it less frequently.

- Christ is present in this ritual in a special way. Some Christians believe the bread and drink become the actual body and blood of Christ. Others believe Christ is present in a spiritual way. But almost all Christians believe this ritual gives God a special opportunity to speak to our spirits and work in our hearts. God speaks through Communion similar to the way He speaks through a sermon, prayer, or Bible reading. But He speaks through Communion in a way that is quite unique as well. It is a very close, loving meeting between Christ and His people—a special kind of rendezvous.

Both sacraments spiritually nourish us for our journey of faith.

Both sacraments spiritually nourish us for our journey of faith. Both deepen our love for Jesus and make us more aware of our continual need for His presence in our lives. Both help us appreciate His sacrifice on the Cross for our salvation. Both unite us more completely with the community of faith as we celebrate God together.

So the next time you participate in a baptismal or Communion service, look for Christ to reveal himself to you in a special, loving way.

Day 30

Remember: Christ gave us two corporate ceremonies to draw us closer to one another and to Him.

While they were eating, Jesus took bread, gave thanks and broke it, and gave it to his disciples, saying, "Take it; this is my body." Then he took the cup, gave thanks and offered it to them, and they all drank from it. "This is my blood of the covenant, which is poured out for many," he said to them (Mark 14:22-24).

Day 31

SIT DOWN AND REST

If you had known what these words mean, "I desire mercy, not sacrifice," you would not have condemned the innocent. For the Son of Man is Lord of the Sabbath (Matt. 12:7-8).

I grew up during a slower time in our culture. On Sunday, people did little more than go to church or sleep in, spend time with family, and enjoy the day with friends and loved ones. Few businesses remained open in our county other than the hospital and an occasional gas station or restaurant. Society offered little competition for our time or attention on our day of rest.

My how times have changed! Unless it happens to be Christmas Day, Sunday is no different from any other business day. The mall is as busy as ever. Children's sports leagues practice and play games, while parents taxi kids and attend sporting events. National sports fill the television schedule on nearly every major network. The phone rings frequently with more things to do than you can possibly schedule.

As Christians, we have one day during the week to continue what God intended as a day of rest—a Sabbath. Saturday served this purpose in biblical times, but Sunday is now our special day. It not only honors Christ's resurrection but also is our Sabbath. So when Scripture says something about the Sabbath, it says some important things about Sunday—the Lord's day.

Our Scripture reading for today finds Jesus addressing the Pharisees on Sabbath observance. They had serious concerns over the activities Jesus and His disciples engaged themselves in on the Sabbath day. Jesus knew Exod. 20:8-10 well, "Remember the Sabbath day by keeping it holy. Six days you shall labor and do all your work, but the seventh day is a Sabbath to the Lord your God. On it you shall not do any work." Jesus reminded the Pharisees of God's original purpose for the regulations regarding the Sabbath as well as all other divine regulations. "I desire mercy, not sacrifice" referred to the many times in the Old Testament when God expressed His desire for His people to live by the spirit, rather than the letter, of the law. God chafes over legalism as much as we do.

That being the case, what best describes the spirit of God's original intention for our Sabbath day? God set one day in seven apart for us to rest from our busy schedules and worship Him. God gave us work to occupy us. Work brings us fulfillment and a sense of accomplishment. God also gave us a time to not work, not think about work, not stress, not live by a to-do list, not rush, and not hurry. Both our body and mind crave times of release from the yokes of responsibility. Even field animals have their yokes removed at the end of the workday, so must we at the end of the workweek.

> *God set one day in seven apart for us to rest*
> *from our busy schedules and worship Him.*

God had our best interests in mind when He created the Sabbath. That's what Jesus meant when He said, "The Sabbath was made for man, not man for the Sabbath" (Mark 2:27). He knows our minds, bodies, and schedules need the rhythms and cycles of labor and rest. Sabbath reminds us:

- To let go
- Of our humanness
- To leave the responsibility of our labors with God for a period of time and let Him watch over our concerns while we rest
- Of our limitedness
- Of the importance of *being* more than *doing*

- To spend significant time with family members
- To care for our mental and physical health
- Of our vital membership in the family of God
- Of the superior value of our spiritual nature
- That our true citizenship is in heaven

As we have discussed so often throughout this book, Christ wants to meet with us in a variety of ways throughout the day. Sadly, we so often preoccupy ourselves with busy schedules that we fail to acknowledge Christ's arrival when He crosses our path. The Sabbath stops our hurry and scurry with a busy schedule to create time and space for Christ to make himself known in inviting ways. What could be a better use of our time than spending it with Christ?

We must not wait until all work is done, until everything on our to-do list is checked off, or until we complete all our household projects. That day may never come! Like weeds in the garden, activities fill our calendar faster than we can accomplish them. God made the Sabbath for us, so when Sunday rolls around each week, stop and take an important break.

Sadly, we so often preoccupy ourselves with busy schedules that we fail to acknowledge Christ's arrival when He crosses our path.

Members of the family of God need the reminders of Sabbath rest as much—if not more—than nonbelievers. We mean well, no doubt, but we find ways to plan so many religious activities on Sunday that it becomes anything but a day of rest and worship of God. The schedule often looks more crowded on Sunday than any other day of the Christian's week. Not good! If this describes your situation, talk together with your small group, pastor, or other spiritual leader about ways to limit programming and responsibilities on Sunday. Guard this time carefully. Reclaim Sunday as the Sabbath—a special gift from God for your physical, mental, emotional, and spiritual well-being. Once you reclaim it, enjoy God's special benefit for you as you make Sabbath a sanctuary for your soul.

Make a special effort next Sabbath day to look for Christ crossing your path as you observe this special day of rest in Him.

Day 31

Remember: God has our best interests in mind when He gives us a day to rest from our labors, worship Him, and enjoy time with family and friends.

For the Son of Man is Lord of the Sabbath (Matt. 12:8).

Day 32

ROADS, GAMES, AND LIFE

Jesus answered, "I am the way and the truth and the life.
No one comes to the Father except through me" (John 14:6).

Roads, airport runways, railways, sports, card games, table games, children's games—what do these items have in common? Rules. What happens if we ignore the rules that regulate each of them? Planes, trains, and automobiles collide. Card, table, and children's games end. Sporting events stall.

Life is like that. We need rules to live by to keep our lives organized and consistent. Our Christian lives in the community of faith also require rules for us to live together. We often refer to these Christian rules of life as a corporate conscience.

By corporate conscience we mean the advice that comes to us from those who have gone before us on the journey of life. Those people learned valuable lessons, and they passed them down to us. Some made bad decisions and have shouted back, "Don't come this way; it's a dead-end road." Others made good decisions and offer their example as a good path to follow. These good and bad decisions create a fund of advice from a large number of people, over a long period of time. We inherit this fund as a Christian community and call it our corporate conscience. But the concept of a corporate conscience has fallen on hard times in recent years. Many no longer seem to care as much about what earlier travelers experienced.

Partly because of the social rebellion of the 1960s and partly because of the cry for personal autonomy, many want to go their own way. Without great care, this spirit of the age can create a spiritual problem for believers. We can reject social convention to the point that

147

rendezvous

we reject God's will for our lives. Corporate conscience gives directives in many areas of life. We do ourselves a favor and avoid heartache when we listen to this conscience. It has our best interests in mind.

In our Scripture reading for today Jesus reminded us that in Him we find our way in life. We are neither experienced enough nor clever enough to live our lives with only our own advice. So we find our way by looking to Jesus, His Word, and the direction He has given other followers. We need the wise counsel of other believers, both from the past and the present, to help guide our steps on the road of life.

Members of the Body of Christ offer a sound contribution to the spiritual rules of life. The following offers a brief summary of the rules from my particular faith community.

1. Follow the directives of the Bible, such as:
   a. Love God with all your heart, soul, mind, and strength, and your neighbor as yourself (Exod. 20:3-6; Mark 12:28-31; Rom. 13:8-10).
   b. Witness to your unsaved friends, inviting them to attend church with you; try to lead them to Christ (Matt. 28:19-20; Rom. 1:14-16; 2 Cor. 5:18-20).
   c. Be courteous to everyone (Eph. 4:32; Titus 3:2; 1 Pet. 2:17; 1 John 3:18).
   d. Be helpful to other Christian believers, in love forbearing one another (Rom. 12:13; Gal. 6:2, 10; Col. 3:12-14).
   e. Seek to do good to the bodies and souls of others; feeding the hungry, clothing the naked, visiting the sick and imprisoned, and ministering to the needy, as opportunity and ability arise (Matt. 25:35-36; 2 Cor. 9:8-10; Gal. 2:10; James 2:15-16; 1 John 3:17-18).
   f. Contribute to the support of the ministry and the church and its work in tithes and offerings (Mal. 3:10; Luke 6:38; 1 Cor. 9:14; 16:2; 2 Cor. 9:6-10).

148

g. Practice the spiritual practices that help you meet Christ, including the public worship of God (Heb. 10:25), the ministry of the Word (Acts 2:42), the sacrament of the Lord's Supper (1 Cor. 11:23-30); searching the Scriptures and meditating on them (Acts 17:11; 2 Tim. 2:15; 3:14-16); family and private devotions (Deut. 6:6-7; Matt. 6:6).

> "[A believer] obeys not from the motive of slavish fear, but on a nobler principle; namely, the grace of God ruling in his heart, and causing all his works to be wrought in love."
> —John Wesley[19]

2. Avoid evil of every kind, including:
   a. Do not take the name of God in vain (Exod. 20:7; James 5:12).
   b. Do not profane the Lord's Day by participation in unnecessary secular activities, so as to indulge in practices that deny its sanctity (Exod. 20:8-11; Isa. 58:13-14; Mark 2:27-28).
   c. Do not participate in sexual immorality, such as premarital or extramarital relations, perversion in any form, or looseness and impropriety of conduct (Exod. 20:14; Matt. 5:27-32; 1 Cor. 6:9-11; Gal. 5:19; 1 Thess. 4:3-7).
   d. Do not adopt habits or practices known to be destructive of physical and mental well-being. Regard your body as a temple of the Holy Spirit (Prov. 20:1; 23:1-3; 1 Cor. 6:17-20; 2 Cor. 7:1; Eph. 5:18).
   e. Do not quarrel, return evil for evil, gossip, slander, or spread surmises injurious to the good names of others (2 Cor. 12:20; Gal. 5:15; Eph. 4:30-32; James 3:5-18; 1 Pet. 3:9-10).
   f. Do not be dishonest, take advantage in buying and selling, bear

false witness, and like works of darkness (Lev. 19:11-18; Rom. 12:17; 1 Cor. 6:7-10).

g. Do not indulge in pride of dress or behavior. Rather, dress with Christian simplicity and modesty (Prov. 29:23; 1 Tim. 2:8-10; 1 Pet. 3:3-4; 1 John 2:15-17).

h. Do not participate in music, literature, and entertainments that dishonor God (1 Cor. 10:31; 2 Cor. 6:14-17; James 4:4).

3. Abide in hearty fellowship with the church, not working against but wholly committed to its doctrines and usages and actively involved in its continuing witness and outreach (Eph. 2:18-22; 4:1-3, 11-16; Phil. 2:1-8; 1 Pet. 2:9-10).[20]

I often hear people complain that they chafe under rules of conduct. But as I look over the above list of rules, I'm hard-pressed to find anything with which to disagree. If anything, they help me live my Christian life better. This list only suggests a few rules for life. Add your own personal insights into Christian living from reading your Bible, listening to the Holy Spirit, and talking with other believers.

As you guide your life with the corporate conscience of your faith community, don't be surprised if you experience Christ in a special way while doing this. Celebrate your efforts as a way to honor the One you love.

Day 32

Remember: Rules help us on the road, with games, and yes even in Christian living.

Jesus answered, "I am the way and the truth and the life. No one comes to the Father except through me" (John 14:6).

Day 33

BETTER TOGETHER

Now when he saw the crowds, he went up on a mountainside and sat down. His disciples came to him, and he began to teach them (Matt. 5:1-2).

Night after night we recently watched television coverage of the devastation that gripped our land as two hurricanes hit the Gulf Coast of the United States. The storms killed people, separated families, destroyed homes, and changed the landscape forever. Many years will pass before complete physical restoration occurs. Many lives will never be fully restored.

During those early weeks of the crisis, I felt a deep stirring in my heart as television news teams featured Christian congregations and entire denominations stepping in to assist individuals. Before the federal government even assessed the situation properly, Christians had already moved quickly to the center of human need. They brought food, water, medicine, cosmetics, clothes, and bedding. Many of them offered spare bedrooms and entire basements to resettle families in their homes. What a picture of the Body of Christ at work in our world!

We have been exploring spiritual practices this week that we do with our faith community. Some of them may also be done by ourselves or with our small group. But these practices take on a different character when done with the whole community. Today we want to look at one more practice that takes on a unique quality with the large group.

In our Bible lesson for today, Jesus sat down with thousands of followers (the whole group) to give them spiritual instruction and direction. The verses you read lead up to the Sermon on the Mount (chaps. 5—7). Jesus talked about many things in this timeless sermon.

He directed us to live and act godly toward others. In different ways, He referenced a spiritual practice we studied last week—hospitality. Let's look at hospitality again today, this time from what happens when the entire group focuses on a single need or problem.

From the Beatitudes at the beginning of the Sermon on the Mount, we see that as members of the Body of Christ we must maintain a posture of humility (5:3), meekness (v. 5), and mercifulness (v. 7). We should offer words and acts of peace (v. 9). We must be willing to accept ridicule and persecution if they come our way (v. 10). We should have an attitude of rejoicing and gladness amid any difficulties coming from our identification with the name and cause of Christ (v. 12). We are to live righteously in all our dealings (v. 20). We must show kindness toward our enemies and those who work against us (vv. 43-48). Our giving to the needy should be done quietly, not for recognition (6:1-4). We must not judge others but leave all judgment to God who knows all of the facts and judges them correctly (7:1-6).

This quick summary certainly does not exhaust the insights on hospitality found in the Sermon on the Mount. It gives us a starting point though. Of all of the gatherings of people in the world, the church should be the most hospitable in the eyes of needy people. We assume a posture of humility, meekness, and mercifulness. We offer words and deeds that promote peace. We expect to be misunderstood and misjudged. We connect all that we do to the cause of Christ.

Of all of the gatherings of people in the world, the church should be the most hospitable in the eyes of needy people.

Having done all of this, we then go on to create space for broken, hurting people to be themselves and find refuge. We share our property, money, time, attention, and concern to meet their needs. We do not require them to make a good impression or create a positive image. We tell them, "Come as you are."

And come they do. I think of examples from my local congregation. We conduct many ministries at our church that reach out to needy people. The never-ending line of those seeking help would quickly bankrupt me as an individual or even my small group. However, when everyone in the entire faith community contributes from what they have, Christ seems to multiply our efforts. Our church offers food, medicine, clothes, school supplies, and several services, such as child care and life skill courses. The supply of goods holds up week after week. It's amazing what Christ can do in a community when all of His followers band together for a common cause.

When I saw the Body of Christ respond in the Gulf Coast following the hurricanes, I could hardly believe the semitrailer loads of relief that arrived day after day. I thrilled over the thousands of helping hands that drove down to help with the cleanup. I could not conceive the millions of dollars in aid offered to the victims. That's because we can never get a clear picture of the load Christians can lift when they lift together.

Our world may threaten us—so much sin, so much brokenness, so much evil. Street drugs, gangs, and violence scare us. We might like to withdraw to our church buildings and sing hymns of praise until we go to be with God in heaven. We might like to insulate and isolate ourselves from all that defiles. But God does not allow the sin, brokenness, and evil to threaten Him. He keeps right on working behind the scenes, offering grace and mercy through His incredible hospitality. He invites His Church to join Him in that hospitality by opening their doors to the needs at hand. He calls us to a corporate life that shares in His ministry to our hurting world. He sends us on a mission every day that is bigger than us or our small group. He urges us to bind together as one large Body of Believers and go into our world to make a difference.

Do we have the strength and ability to accomplish what needs to be done? No, we do not. It's not in knowing we have the ability; it's in knowing we do not that we find strength. You see, when we realize the job is much too big for us, we depend on Him. He then works through us to supply what is lacking and gets the job done. He only requires a willing heart that's dependent on Him.

Yes, hospitality takes on a whole new quality when practiced by the entire faith community. We're better together! So let's join in and create a safe environment where Jesus' power can flow. Let's live a Sermon on the Mount life. We might find that in the midst of our efforts, we have a surprising and fresh encounter with Jesus.

Day 33

Remember: God can do more through you when you minister through the larger Body of Christ than He can when you operate by yourself or only with your small group.

Now when he saw the crowds, he went up on a mountainside and sat down. His disciples came to him, and he began to teach them (Matt. 5:1-2).

How may we resemble God,

His genuine children prove?

Jesus, Thou the way hast showed

In universal love.

Let Thy love implanted be,

Pure, impartial, unconfined;

Then mankind in us shall see

The Father of mankind.

—Charles Wesley[21]

ENCOUNTERING CHRIST IN
THE WORLD

rendezvous

Day 34

AN EXAMPLE

You are the salt of the earth. . . . You are the light of the world (Matt. 5:13-14).

Up to this point we have considered spiritual practices that help us see Christ daily in new ways. We have looked at these practices in four different social settings: alone, with a close friend, in a small group of friends, and in a faith community. All of these settings have at least one thing in common: they allow us to stay in our comfort zone most of the time. The warmth and acceptance of our Christian friends invite us to remain with them. But we must resist the temptation to stay there.

Jesus challenged us yesterday to live a Sermon on the Mount life. Neither His example nor His directives give us permission to hide in isolation from the world. He ventured out into His world. We must follow His example and venture out into our world as well. We must be all God needs us to be as we live a Christian example in our world.

We must follow His example and venture out into our world.

In our Scripture reading for today, taken from the Sermon on the Mount, Jesus referred to us as salt and light in our world. What do those images say about what God has in mind for us as we live for Him in our world? Salt has a unique flavor. It preserves meat. It gives food a better taste. It disinfects by killing germs. And it makes people thirsty.

We Christians can have these same qualities as we live in our world. We have a different viewpoint from our world because we live by a different value system. We offer a unique flavor to the atmo-

159

sphere at school, work, and in the neighborhood. We preserve our world the same way a few righteous inhabitants of Sodom could have preserved it from judgment (see Gen. 18:16-33). We bring a better taste to every situation with our positive and hopeful view on life. Our personal ethics should be so clean that everyone who knows us knows we live an upright life. Our example should make people thirst to know what makes us different and to want to be like us.

In Jesus' day salt lost its flavor when it fell on the ground or came in contact with rain or too much sun. Like salt falling to the ground, we, too, can lose our spiritual vigor by taking on the world's bad habits or getting caught up in worldly thinking. Like exposure to rain and sun, we, too, can lose our spiritual vigor by letting the natural stresses and strains of life get to us and simply water us down or wear us out. We cannot allow either of these negative influences to sap us. As Jesus said, if we let that happen, we become ineffective for Kingdom building.

What qualities of light might Jesus have had in mind for His followers? Light does not produce itself; it comes from a source. It illuminates our surroundings. It produces heat. It generates power.

All of these qualities also relate to the spiritual effect we should have in our world. We never produce our own spiritual light; we only reflect God's light as we live in close personal relationship with Him. Our spiritual influence should light a path to God for those who do not know Him. The light of our influence develops as we participate in the spiritual practices we have discussed in this book. Our lives should exhibit a spiritual power that can be explained only as God's work.

In Matt. 5:14-16, Jesus named three locations for light: home, city, and world. A lamp's light reaches only one room of a private home. Many homes together create a city; the light of an entire city can be seen for miles. The light of the sun far exceeds a city's light and spreads across the whole world. Notice how the light's influence grows with each enlarged area. Jesus reminded us in this analogy that our spiritual influence begins at home with the people who see us the most and know us best. We must first be a good Christian example at home. From there our influence reaches our friends, small group, and faith community. As we live a good example in all of these arenas, our spiritual influence reaches beyond these borders to our world.

The world may not be as warm and inviting as our Christian fellowship, but Christ sends us out anyway.

This week we are going to look at ways we relate as Christians to our world. We will expand what we started yesterday in our discussion of Christian hospitality. The world may not be as warm and inviting as our Christian fellowship, but Christ sends us out anyway. He does not send us alone, however. In His last extended conversation with His disciples in John 17:14-18, He prayed a prayer of protection for them and us in this important assignment. In the midst of that prayer He said, "My prayer is not that you take them out of the world but that you protect them from the evil one" (v. 15).

Christ sends you to be an example to your world and to minister in His name. Thus you may expect that He will come to be with you and minister to you as you follow His lead. Learn to watch for Him as you venture out into your world.

Day 34

Remember: Rather than withdrawing from our world, Christ calls us to be salt and light in it as we live lives that represent Him well.

You are the salt of the earth. . . . You are the light of the world (Matt. 5:13-14).

Day 35

A LOOK, A WORD, A TOUCH

A man with leprosy came to him and begged him on his knees, "If you are willing, you can make me clean." Filled with compassion, Jesus reached out his hand and touched the man. "I am willing," he said. "Be clean!" Immediately the leprosy left him and he was cured (Mark 1:40-42).

A few years ago our family experienced a very unusual expression of compassion. We were taking a vacation through Colorado with our camper in tow and having a wonderful time together. Then without warning the axle broke loose from the camper frame. We found ourselves stranded along the side of the road. I walked to a nearby house and called a wrecker to come and tow our camper into the next town.

That's when the mystery began. The wrecker driver dropped our disabled camper at a repair shop but refused to take payment for his services. The repairman worked overtime and built a new axle bracket but charged us much less than its value. Because the repair took an extra day, we stayed overnight in a local motel. The motel clerk only charged us half the room rate. The next morning we ate breakfast at a restaurant next to the motel. The manager knew why we spent the night in his town and refused to let us pay for our breakfast.

By that point, I had to know what was going on with these people showing such kindness to total strangers. Back at the repair shop, I described what had happened to us over the past 24 hours. The mechanic explained, "We experienced some tough economic times when the only factory in town closed last year. We know what it feels like to be down on your luck. We're doing better now. So when we see someone in need, we're quick to lend a helping hand."

Now that's Exhibit No. 1 for compassion. Jesus gave us another example of compassion when He healed the man with the horrible skin disease in our Scripture lesson. This example could be multiplied a dozen times throughout Jesus' ministry. He saw a man who everyone else looked past. He reached out to this untouchable man. He offered compassion to an outcast and healed him.

Anyone who wants to follow Jesus must follow His lead in showing compassion to the needy of our world. He illustrated this point with the parable of the good Samaritan (Luke 10:25-37). Read this parable again if you have not read it lately. It offers important reminders about involving ourselves compassionately in our world.

Anyone who wants to follow Jesus must follow His lead in showing compassion to the needy of our world.

Through His example and parables Jesus gives us an action plan for our lives. He wants us to reach out in compassion and become healing agents to hurting people in our world. He wants us to see people no one else sees. But more than just seeing them, He wants us to reach out to people no one else reaches out to. He wants us to go out of our way and take time for those who are battered and broken. He wants us to offer help to these hurting people in His name. Taken together, He wants us to be His hands and His feet, continuing His work on earth as we take His compassion to those who need it most.

So, what can we do? We first must ask Jesus to help us see our needy world as He sees it. We must ask Him to help us look at it through His eyes. Then we must depend on Him to work through us to minister to the needs He shows us. From there, the list of ways to get involved is almost endless:

- We pray for and with those who need God's help.
- We seek to connect needs with answers.
- We develop a keen eye to see those who need an encouraging word and give it to them.

- We support those around us who are struggling with personal, vocational, emotional, relational, or spiritual problems.
- We extend to others the same mercy and grace Jesus extended to us.
- We tend to the needs of the sick, hospitalized, homebound, and disenfranchised.
- We come alongside and offer a helping hand to those who are laboring under a heavy load.
- We offer our time, money, energy, or a listening ear to anyone who needs it.

In it all, we treat needy people with dignity and respect. The attitudes of humility, meekness, and mercifulness that we discussed last week from the Sermon on the Mount (Day 33) prevent us from thinking of ourselves as somehow superior to those we are helping. For Christian compassion to remain truly Christian, we must properly view ourselves as fellow recipients of God's help. We offer fellow travelers a hand as we pass God's blessing along to them.

> "Neighbourliness is not a quality in other people, it is simply their claim on ourselves. Every moment and every situation challenges us to action and to obedience. We have literally no time to sit down and ask ourselves whether so-and-so is our neighbour or not. We must get into action and obey—we must behave like a neighbour to him."
>
> —Dietrich Bonhoeffer[22]

I will never forget the comment made by a homeless man who came to speak to my ethics class at the university a few years ago. During our conversation together in front of the class, I asked him, "What do you most desire from these students?" I expected him to ask for

164

money, food, or clothes. Instead he said, "I would like to be treated with the dignity that every human being deserves." Wow! Could it be that one of the greatest gifts we can give people is the respect they deserve as God's special creations?

Jesus demonstrated compassion as a daily lifestyle throughout His life on earth. It was second nature for Him to show compassion. He urged His followers to live the same way. Read Jesus' sobering account of the sheep and the goats in Matt. 25:31-46. One of the more subtle truths in this passage is in verses 37-39 with the words, "Lord, when did we see you hungry and feed you, or thirsty and give you something to drink? When did we see you a stranger and invite you in, or needing clothes and clothe you? When did we see you sick or in prison and go to visit you?" The acts of compassion by these disciples of Jesus became such a natural part of their lives that they did not even notice they were doing them. That's the way Jesus wants all of His followers to live.

Jesus demonstrated compassion as a daily lifestyle throughout His life on earth.

Christian compassion expresses itself in as many different ways as human need expresses itself. Perhaps you show it best when you daily offer a look, a word, or a touch in Jesus' name to everyone you connect with in your world. Every so often look back over your acts of compassion. Can you tell which of the people you assisted was Jesus (Matt. 25:40)?

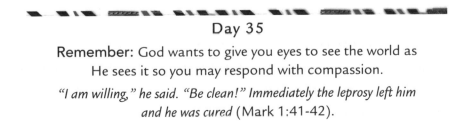

Day 35

Remember: God wants to give you eyes to see the world as He sees it so you may respond with compassion.

"I am willing," he said. "Be clean!" Immediately the leprosy left him and he was cured (Mark 1:41-42).

165

Day 36

GET LOST

If anyone comes to me and does not hate his father and mother, his wife and children, his brothers and sisters—yes, even his own life—he cannot be my disciple (Luke 14:26).

One of the most difficult transitions for my wife and me occurred five years into our pastoral ministry. We both loved the tasks God gave us and planned to remain at them for the rest of our lives. Then we sensed His call to go back to school and get more education. Why? I thought I had all of the formal education I needed to pastor. The more we prayed about it, the more we sensed Him calling us in this new direction.

So we fearfully resigned our pastoral assignment, packed all of our possessions into a moving van, and headed back to school. Just when I thought I had a clear sense of direction for the path my life would take, I was lost on a road that cost me a career I loved dearly and promised nothing as fulfilling in the future. I know I was foolish to feel that way, but I did. Four years plus many tests and term papers later, I completed two more academic degrees and found myself at my new task. More than two decades have passed since that transition, and I'm still at the same job—training young men and women at the university level to be ministers of the gospel of Jesus Christ. I absolutely love the new assignment God gave me!

In our Scripture passage for today, Jesus urges us to sit down and count the cost of following Him. He catches our attention fast by telling us to hate all of our relatives and ourselves. Now, Jesus does not actually want us to hate our relatives and ourselves. He knows that love is unquestioned. But our affection for and devotion to Him must be so far above that level of love that it pales in comparison. These other loves must offer no competition to our love and devotion to Christ.

Jesus says we should not enter into discipleship with Him lightly. He does not want us to accept His call, then later feel we have been led astray or tricked. He does not want us to think we can get by with a partial commitment. He tells us up front that He will require everything of us. He says plainly in verse 33, "Any of you who does not give up everything he has cannot be my disciple."

Why bring up the matter of total commitment on a week when we are discussing spiritual practices we exercise in the world? Because all of the things we have discussed so far this week and all of the things we will explore in the remainder of this book can only be done properly if we live a lifestyle totally committed to God's will and way.

It is easy to be a good Christian example when we venture out into our world for limited periods. We can then withdraw from the world and enjoy our private lives. It is much more demanding to be a good example when we live a life of total commitment that is on display in our world 24/7. It is easy to perform acts of compassion once in a while. It is much more demanding to live a lifestyle of compassion daily.

When you first read this passage of Scripture, it sounds as if Jesus is calling us to a decision. He is. Yet, at another level, He is calling us to something much more. He is directing us to an action plan for our daily lives. This action plan makes us continually available to do God's work in our world whenever He calls on us.

This action plan makes us continually available to do God's work in our world whenever He calls on us.

Once we settle our commitment to discipleship, we're ready for Him to deploy us into our needy world. He will think of dozens of things for us to do once we have established our commitment. Jesus' instruction in this passage calls us to a lifestyle in which we give up our own plans and directions to follow Him.

"Say, 'Yes, Lord, YES!' to everything, and trust Him so to work in you to will as to bring your whole wishes and affections into conformity with His own sweet, and lovable, and most lovely will."
—Hannah Whitall Smith (1832—1911)[23]

Notice that this passage about the cost of discipleship immediately precedes Jesus' parables of a lost sheep, a lost coin, and a lost son (see Luke 15). You have no doubt heard more than one sermon take those parables to be pictures of God searching for spiritually lost humanity. The parables certainly tell us that. But what if Jesus also had something else in mind when He told those parables? Maybe those parables depict a lifestyle that abandons personal plans and directions in favor of something more compelling. The shepherd (vv. 1-7) forgot about everything else as he went searching for one lost sheep. The woman (vv. 8-10) stopped her daily routine and turned her house upside down looking for a lost coin. The father (vv. 11-32) thought of nothing other than getting his lost son back home. All three parables tell of people consumed with a passion that took complete control of their lives. They call us to a lifestyle of equal abandonment.

Today's spiritual practice puts us on call for God's special deployment as we live in the world. I have several friends who work jobs that place them on call certain days of the week. These doctors, nurses, and factory mechanics carry pagers or cell phones at all times while on call. They go about their normal routine until a pager buzzes or a phone rings. Then they drop everything and attend to the need.

What a way to live in our world as a follower of Jesus Christ! We go about our normal routines, but with the awareness that we're available to do whatever job He has for us whenever He needs us to do it.

Jesus addresses the outcome of this lifestyle in John 12:25: "The man who loves his life will lose it, while the man who hates his life in this world will keep it for eternal life." What a paradox! Human reason tells us that we make the most of life by keeping personal control of it. Jesus says we make the most of our lives by getting lost in His will, way, and work. In the end, He will give us eternal life for our commitment.

So go out into your world today and live on call to do His bidding. He's sure to give you something to do. As you give yourself in this open-ended manner, you are likely to see Jesus in a brand-new light!

Day 36

Remember: You are on call for God's special deployment at all times.

*If anyone comes to me and does not hate his father and mother,
his wife and children, his brothers and sisters—yes, even his own life—
he cannot be my disciple* (Luke 14:26).

Day 37

AN INVITATION FROM JESUS

And anyone who does not carry his cross and follow me cannot be my disciple
(Luke 14:27).

Yesterday we talked about being on call for God 24/7. Our world has seen that lifestyle from Mother Teresa and people like her. God's on-call people see human need and pour their lives into lending a helping hand, in Jesus' name. God has them strategically scattered globally. They minister in metropolitan cities and rural villages. They work on mountains and in valleys, on islands and mainlands. They go where God's love sends them and stay as long as a job calls them. I've watched friends from college, university students, and fellow believers at church live this on-call lifestyle. This lifestyle is not a weekend project or an occasional hobby; it consumes their priorities on a daily basis.

Today's Bible reading follows yesterday's. It continues Jesus' thought. After urging us to sit down and count the cost of discipleship, He says this lifestyle is about carrying a cross. What do you suppose He meant by that? At the time Jesus spoke these words, His disciples saw the cross as a torturous form of death for criminals and political prisoners. After Jesus' own death on the Cross, they realized these words called them to the same life of humility and submission that Jesus had lived. They did not know it at the time, but Jesus was giving His disciples an example to follow.

Jesus' reference to cross-bearing reminds us that living for Him in this world may carry a high price tag. It involves hardship and suffering. There's that word *suffering* again. We discussed suffering as a spiritual discipline on Day 19 when we talked about sharing the burden of another person. We also discussed it on Day 26 as a ministry of small groups. But suffering takes on an entirely different quality when we minister out in the world.

Sometimes we find that we suffer as a direct result of our commitment to Christ or as we minister in His name. This may be what Paul had in mind when he said, "Now I rejoice in what was suffered for you, and I fill up in my flesh what is still lacking in regard to Christ's afflictions, for the sake of his body, which is the church" (Col. 1:24). Paul in no way implies here that Jesus' atoning sacrifice on the Cross needed his additional effort to be complete. Jesus paid the full and complete price for our salvation.

> "Discipleship means allegiance to the suffering Christ, and it is therefore not at all surprising that Christians should be called upon to suffer. In fact it is a joy and a token of his grace. . . . In the hour of the cruellest torture [Christian martyrs] bear for his sake, they are made partakers in the perfect joy and bliss of fellowship with him."
> —Dietrich Bonhoeffer[24]

Paul is telling us that in following Jesus in Christian ministry, he suffered for preaching the gospel. Christ became Paul's example. Paul continued in the worthy tradition of Christ's suffering on the Cross by experiencing the continuation of that suffering in getting the message to the world. He wrote these words from prison and felt a great sense of honor that his suffering could further the gospel message and bring more people to Christ.

Paul becomes an example for us. We, too, can share in the sufferings of Christ as we proclaim the good news of the gospel message to our world. It just may be that, like Paul, we will be called upon to suffer because of our Christian commitment. God may then use that suffering to further His work on earth.

We may also find a ministry of suffering in our world when we come alongside those who suffer and lighten their load. Everything we said on Days 19 and 26 about suffering with a fellow believer also applies to suffering with those who do not yet know Jesus. We may suffer when we share in ministries of compassion to our world or when we get lost in Christ's service when He calls us to an especially difficult task. Circumstances will change with every situation. But suffering with hurting people is a similar ministry in every culture of the world.

This discussion can sound so formal and academic. It's not. It's very practical, because Jesus calls us to follow His lead in cross-bearing. That is, we must be willing to suffer whatever we need to suffer to get the gospel message to our world. The suffering may be because of our proclamation or because we are sharing in the burdens of hurting people. Either way, we gladly suffer because Christ has called us to this ministry.

We must be willing to suffer whatever we need to suffer to get the gospel message to our world.

Have you experienced any suffering at work, school, or home because you identify with Christ? Would you experience suffering if you identified even more fully than you do now? Have you come alongside someone in your world and helped with a load and in so doing perhaps suffered with him or her? How might you do a better job with this type of ministry?

All of these questions remind us that our interaction as a Christian in our world may cause discomfort—discomfort that may be occasional or long-lasting. But that should not surprise us. Jesus warned us it would happen. His ministry led to a cross; ours will as well. Like

Paul, we must rejoice that Jesus counts us worthy to suffer for His sake. Remember, when you suffer for Christ, He suffers with you.

When times of suffering come your way from living a Christian life in the world, be watchful. You will meet Jesus right in the midst of your suffering!

Day 37

Remember: Jesus left us an invitation to join Him in His suffering as we minister in our world.

And anyone who does not carry his cross and follow me cannot be my disciple (Luke 14:27).

Day 38

THE BATTLE FOR JUSTICE

This was to fulfill what was spoken through the prophet Isaiah: "Here is my servant whom I have chosen, the one I love, in whom I delight; I will put my Spirit on him, and he will proclaim justice to the nations. He will not quarrel or cry out; no one will hear his voice in the streets. A bruised reed he will not break, and a smoldering wick he will not snuff out, till he leads justice to victory. In his name the nations will put their hope" (Matt. 12:17-21).

"That's not fair!" Remember the first time you said that? It probably takes you back to your childhood when you compared your punishment to that of a brother or sister. Or maybe on the elementary school playground you felt the teacher favored another child over you. Situations differ, but all of us have made that declaration with extreme feeling. What's more, I'll bet you've even said it more than a few times since becoming an adult.

Comparisons between the way things are and the way things should be enter daily into our conversations. These comparisons remind us that God has hardwired us with an awareness of how He wants people treated in His world. People are not always treated the way He wants them treated. When that happens, we know it. We say, "That's not fair."

> *God has hardwired us with an awareness of how He wants people treated in His world.*

Perhaps without even realizing it, we offer our testimony to the significance of justice. *Justice* sounds like such an impersonal word. It conjures images of courtrooms, lawyers, and judges. Those images are

174

accurate, but justice is more, much more. Justice is always personal, for it involves people. It calls us to love others as we seek their good, their protection, and their fair treatment. It urges us to do all we can to correct the injustice of institutions, organizations, businesses, systems, and societies that belittle or harm people. It challenges us to call for fairness toward all people. It invites us to join in the fight to make our world just, right, and fair.

Our Scripture reading for today echoes the prophecy of Isa. 42:1-4. Isaiah saw a day when the Messiah would bring justice to our world. Matthew picked up on this vision and saw its fulfillment in Jesus Christ. The Hebrew people of Jesus' day looked for a military leader to sweep in and bring them justice through military conquest. Jesus fulfilled the vision but as a quiet and gentle conqueror (v. 19), not one making a great commotion with loud noise in the streets. Jesus usually withdrew from head-on conflict with religious leaders. In fact, He conducted much of His ministry in the countryside. His message got back to town, however, and began to change everything. He brought about a quiet revolution that changed His world before most people even realized it.

Notice in verse 18 that Jesus came to proclaim the message of justice to our world. Pay particular attention to the two images in verse 20. A bruised reed speaks of broken, hurting people whom the world has forgotten and passed by. They are without homes, jobs, health, or hope. They are the marginalized of society, fragile and easily destroyed. Jesus cares deeply for them and will not destroy them. A smoldering wick pictures an old-fashioned oil lamp that has run out of fuel. The flame has already died; the wick is about to lose what little fire it has left. The wick represents people who have reached the end of their resources. Jesus will restore them and breathe new life back into them.

Jesus came to our world to make justice victorious. By His hand it will ultimately triumph. He came to rescue the oppressed, deliver the imprisoned, heal the sick, meet the needs of those who hurt, and show people the way to a relationship with the Father. Jesus is the hope of all nations (v. 21). He is our hope as well.

Jesus came to our world to make justice victorious.

Isaiah had a glorious vision of a preferred future with the coming Messiah. Matthew saw the vision fulfilled in his day. The call for justice in this vision did not end with Jesus' ministry on earth, however. When He returned to His Father, He left His followers with the challenge to carry on the work that He started. So, now here we are in our day and the need for justice lingers on. What shall we do? Shall we lament that the vision has not reached its complete fulfillment? Or shall we roll up our sleeves and pick up the challenge to carry on with the example Jesus left us?

We, the community of faith, are the Body of Christ in the world. We are His hands and His feet. As we said yesterday, we must pick up His cross and follow Him (Luke 14:27). Each of us must join Him in His battle for justice. What can one person do against the unjust systems of our world? A great deal. Remember Jesus' quiet revolution. This revolution requires our daily involvement.

- It urges us to ask God to give us eyes to see the injustice all around us as He sees it. We must look for it every day. When we find it, we must seek ways to bring change.
- It calls us to treat every person we meet impartially and fairly.
- It challenges us to be good stewards of all of our resources: time, energy, influence, money, and so forth.
- It invites us to join in just causes in our community wherever we see people misused or oppressed.
- It asks us to share our time, money, and self with poor or needy people we know.
- It requests that we not buy products from companies that ex-

ploit their workers, underpay them, or fail to provide a safe work environment.

- It challenges us to live sacrificially so we can share in the fight for justice.

Jesus came to our world with a message of deliverance and hope. He opened a way for us to fellowship with the Father. In so doing, He brought the kingdom of God to us. We possess citizenship in that Kingdom. As citizens of the Kingdom, Jesus invites us to join Him in bringing justice to our world. Individually, with God's help, we can do a lot—remember what Jesus did—but together we can do so much more. We can make a worldwide difference.

Think of tangible ways you can join Christ today in the battle for justice in our world. As you do, look for Him to assist you in your efforts. Remember, "For I, the LORD, love justice" (Isa. 61:8).

Day 38

Remember: Christ came to bring justice to our world; He invites us to join Him in this vision.

And he will proclaim justice to the nations (Matt. 12:18).

Day 39

PROCLAIM THE GOOD NEWS

These twelve Jesus sent out with the following instructions: "Do not go among the Gentiles or enter any town of the Samaritans. Go rather to the lost sheep of Israel. As you go, preach this message: 'The kingdom of heaven is near'" (Matt. 10:5-7).

To help my university students learn how to apply ministry principles to real-life situations, I sometimes take them on outings. For example, to give students a feel for evangelism I have taken them into the community to talk to people in their homes and in public parks about Jesus. Talking to strangers may not be as effective as witnessing to family members, friends, or neighbors, but it helps the students get more comfortable about sharing their faith with people they meet.

Jesus sent His disciples on an outing in this passage of Scripture. Matthew 10 records His instructions for this outing along with the message He wanted His disciples to proclaim. They were to announce, "The kingdom of heaven is near" (v. 7). Along with this proclamation, the disciples were to offer several compassionate ministries (v. 8*a*). As we have so often discussed in this book, their model for ministry came from Jesus himself. He extended grace and mercy along with salvation to His followers, and they were to offer this same grace, mercy, and salvation to those they met (v. 8*b*).

We learn several things about witnessing for Jesus from this outing. First, wherever His disciples went, they were to make friends with people who received the gospel message and stay in their homes (v. 11). The disciples no doubt reaffirmed the importance of a community of faith. The Early Church from its inception was community based.

Second, Jesus instructed them to stay with their original host in each town (v. 11). They were not to move to a more comfortable or socially advanced home. Followers of Jesus must never get consumed with striving after physical comforts or social standing.

Third, this outing required the disciples to depend on others for their needs (vv. 9-10). It taught them that following Jesus would never lead to wealth. He did not want them to think His ways led to a get-rich-quick scheme. It also forced them to rely completely on God to supply their needs. This important lesson proved beneficial to the Early Church as it learned to depend on God's Spirit after Jesus returned to the Father.

From this instructive outing, we see that evangelism starts with a simple message: "The kingdom of heaven is near." It was near in Jesus' day because He lived among us. It is near today because the Holy Spirit lives in us. Jesus brought God's kingdom to earth in ways unlike any the world had ever known.

Evangelism brings converts, and this leads to faith communities. These faith communities provide people with spiritual families that unite them to one another and God. New converts grow spiritually as they continue to belong to the spiritual family. Spiritual growth has been the subject of this book. Today's lesson reminds us that evangelism adds to our numbers, renews the community of faith, and starts the cycle all over again for growing a new generation of Christians.

Members of a community of faith are better together than apart. They speak wholeness into one another's lives. They strengthen and support one another. They grow together in Christ as they become His Body in the world.

So often the very mention of the word *evangelism* scares believers. They think they have to memorize a theological defense of the Christian faith or be prepared to answer every conceivable question someone might throw at them. Not to fear. Jesus reminds us that evangelism simply means declaring the gospel. He has already spent time with the people we meet. He has gone before us through the Holy Spirit and prepared the way. All we have to do is tell them the Good News.

So when you talk to someone new, try to discover what God has been doing in his or her life. Listen to the person's story and find ways to tie it to the gospel. If you have an opening, tell the person what Jesus has done for you. But don't be pushy; let God guide you. Above all, let the person know you really care about him or her. Don't leave the impression that he or she is just another notch on your evangelism belt. Remember, not everyone will respond with one contact. A person often comes to Christ over time through a trusting relationship. You may not win a certain individual to Christ, but someone else might because you continued to care.

If your conversation goes well with a person, he or she may have some questions for you. Think carefully about your response but also allow the Holy Spirit to work in the moment. Some questions you can answer easily; others may take time. Let the person know what you can answer and what you can't. Here are some questions you may be asked:

- Why do we suffer if God loves us?
- Who is Jesus Christ?
- Why are you a Christian?
- How do you explain all the suffering that has been caused in the name of religion? Of Christ?
- What does it mean to have faith in Jesus?
- How did you come to know Jesus?
- How do you cope when the troubles of life close in on you?
- Why do you have such a positive outlook on life?
- Where is your hope?

Evangelism means simply declaring the gospel.

Questions about how you met Jesus and how knowing Him has changed your life are among the best and easiest to answer. When you get the chance, tell the person all you can, openly and sincerely. Let him or her know that being with Jesus really does make a difference.

We find a good example of a person doing this very thing in John

9. Jesus healed a man in the early part of the chapter. The Pharisees gathered to investigate the incident. They believed Jesus violated their laws with this healing. The man's parents refused to involve themselves in the inquiry, because they feared they would lose worship privileges at the Temple. They insisted that the man speak for himself. They asked the man a number of leading questions on two separate occasions, and as we will see, he gave a powerful response.

Notice what the healed man did. He refused to get caught up in theological arguments, he refused to side with the Pharisees, and he refused to remain silent. He did what we all can do—he told what he knew. He shared his personal experience in his own words. His account had no drama and very little detail. It emphasized the central message: Jesus' touch! I love the way he cut through all of the intellectual gymnastics of the Pharisees with his simple statement, "I was blind but now I see!" (v. 25).

We can all proclaim the gospel to our world. The Holy Spirit has prepared the way. We just have to link to the gospel what God is already doing in the lives of people. That often means listening, caring, and telling what Jesus has done for us. The story of Christ's work in our lives is too exciting not to relate! We don't have to be effervescent and dramatic. We just have to be real. People care more about us being genuine than they do about hearing a grandiose tale.

So be alert to how Christ is preparing the hearts of others and tell them what He has done for you. He will bless you for sharing. You will, no doubt, find that you see Christ in enriching ways as you participate in this spiritual practice.

Day 39

Remember: Few of us are called to be professional evangelists; all of us are called to be witnesses.

The kingdom of heaven is near (Matt. 10:7).

Day 40

PASS IT ON

Therefore go and make disciples of all nations, baptizing them in the name of the Father and of the Son and of the Holy Spirit, and teaching them to obey everything I have commanded you. And surely I am with you always, to the very end of the age (Matt. 28:19-20).

We talked yesterday about the important ministry of evangelism to our world. We said that evangelism adds to our numbers, renews the community of faith, and starts the cycle all over again of growing a new generation of Christians. Today we want to pick up that thought again and add to it. We cannot just win converts to Jesus Christ, as important as that is. We must also assimilate these new converts into the community of faith the way we bring newborn babies home from the hospital and assimilate them into the family.

In these closing verses of Matthew's Gospel, Jesus does two important things. First, He commissions His apostles and us to spread the gospel message throughout the world and make disciples (vv. 19-20*a*). Second, He promises to be with us every day of our lives (v. 20*b*).

In verse 19 Jesus shares some of His authority with His disciples. This includes not only the disciples present with Jesus that day but also all disciples of Jesus yet to come. That includes you and me in our generation. In essence Jesus deputizes us to participate with Him in getting the word out about God's plan of salvation. We receive our commission to join Jesus in disciple making. This commission goes out not just to pastors, evangelists, and missionaries but to all followers of Jesus Christ. We all have a role to play in disciple making.

God assigns different roles to His followers, such as apostles, prophets, evangelists, pastors, and teachers (Eph. 4:11). Paul lists many other roles in 1 Cor. 12:7-11 and Rom. 12:6-8. These roles differ among us because of our individual gifts, talents, abilities, and personalities. God made us all different. He uses each of us in our own unique way to contribute to the growth of His kingdom. That's why Paul takes extra effort in verses 12-31 to explain the importance of recognizing and coordinating our various strengths and weaknesses. Look over these lists and decide what gifts God has given you.

In our Scripture passage for today, however, Jesus gives a commission to all of us. He challenges each of us to

- Go
- Make disciples in all nations
- Baptize them into the faith
- Teach them the doctrines and lifestyle of Christ's followers

In the last part of verse 20, Jesus promises to be with us. Matthew began and ended his book with this reminder. He started in 1:23 by calling Mary's child "Immanuel," which means "God with us." This title is a signal of Jesus' coming to earth to live among us. In 28:20 Jesus extends His presence to us even after He returns to heaven. He promises to remain by our side for as long as we live. He fulfilled that promise by sending us the Holy Spirit (John 14:18 and Acts 2:1-4).

Jesus charges every word in this passage with an urgent challenge. Notice how He balances His great challenge to go into all the world and make disciples with a great promise to boost our courage. We do not go into the world alone. We do not devise our own plans. We do not create our own strategies. With the aid of the Holy Spirit, we face the challenge to make disciples by receiving the direction and strength from Christ himself! He's our Companion, Guide, Confidant, and Friend. Partnering together with the Creator of the universe to make disciples for His kingdom—what a challenge!

Jesus' promise to be at our side applies not just to our difficult days or our heavy ministry days but also to every day! Sure, we expect Christ to draw near to us when we are being tempted, tried, persecuted, or challenged because of our faith. But Jesus says He will be with us on our great days and even our run-of-the-mill days. Now that's a Friend who sticks closer than a brother or sister. He'll be with us right until we cross over to the other side; then He'll welcome us through eternity's door.

Today concludes our study of a few of the many ways we can get involved in our world. We hardly scratched the surface of the many things we can do to intersect our hurting world with the hope of Christ. We talked about the importance of letting our light shine and being a good example in the world. We spoke of developing eyes like God's eyes to see the needs of hurting humanity and about responding with hands of compassion. We emphasized the importance of being on call 24/7 for God's special deployment. We reminded ourselves that being an ambassador for Jesus in the world often means suffering. That does not deter us, however. We carry on with His work, attempting to bring justice to all who need it.

Involvement in our world goes beyond compassionate ministry and social service, however. Of all the ways Christ wants us to get involved in our world, our most important work is helping people to know Him and accept His good news. Once people do this and decide to join the faith community, we disciple them in what it means to be part of the family of God.

Of all the ways Christ wants us to get involved in our world, our most important work is helping people to know Him and accept His good news.

You play a vital role in discipling new believers. It can be hard work. Yet in the midst of the challenge you will find that Christ comes to you not only to resource you for the task but also to fellowship with you as you carry it out. Always remember Jesus' closing words from our text, "Surely I am with you always."

Day 40

Remember: Jesus invites us to join Him in making disciples for the next generation of the community of faith.

Therefore go and make disciples (Matt. 28:19).

CONCLUSION
HABITS OF THE HEART

Everything I have said in this book centers on this closing thought: All of the spiritual practices and exercises we have explored flow from our love life with Christ. We do them as a natural response to the love we share, not because we feel compelled to follow a prescribed spiritual routine.

Every morning I make a cup of coffee for my wife. I developed this habit not because she demands it of me or because I'm trying to impress her. I make her a daily cup of coffee because I love her. The habit flows naturally from my love for her. It becomes one more way of saying, "I cherish our relationship together."

We have looked at several spiritual practices and exercises in this book. Please do not think of them as just more tasks to add to your already busy schedule. Think of them as more ways to express the love you share with Christ and as new ways to encounter Him in your life. I'm convinced Christ comes to us in a variety of ways every day. We must keep our eyes open for those opportunities so we can rendezvous with Him. Our desire to be with Him will grow with every meeting. And our time together will become the best part of the day.

Encountering Christ daily has a wonderful effect on us: The more we are with Him, the more we become like Him. Yes, we grow in Christlikeness as we live in relationship with Him. But as I said in the introduction, we must never make Christlikeness our only goal. Rather, it flows as a by-product of our love relationship with Him. Although our time with Him in our daily rendezvous leaves us looking more and more like Him, it is being with Him and loving Him that is most important of all.

The life Christ displayed when He lived on this earth naturally flowed from the love He shared with His Father. Christ's character and conduct resulted from the habits of His heart, not a prescribed list of dos and don'ts. By habits of the heart I mean the things He did naturally because of His heart's desires. Like Christ, we, too, can develop our spiritual exercises into habits that flow naturally from the desires of our heart. Our chief desire should be to love Christ supremely and follow Him completely.

Let me leave you with a few verses of Scripture that remind us of this important truth. Paul summarized it well in 2 Cor. 3:18, "And we, who with unveiled faces all reflect the Lord's glory, are being transformed into his likeness with ever-increasing glory, which comes from the Lord, who is the Spirit." Imagine yourself transformed by the power of God as you live in daily relationship with Christ! Peter explains the way God performs this transformation. He says He does it as we participate in Christ's divine nature. "Through these he has given us his very great and precious promises, so that through them you may participate in the divine nature and escape the corruption in the world caused by evil desires" (2 Pet. 1:4).

Here's our challenge. Rather than trying to decide which spiritual exercise or practice will help us become more Christlike, we must make Christ part of everything we do. We must bring Him into our words, our thoughts, our actions, our reactions, our work, our leisure, everything. Then we must depend on His Spirit to work His transforming miracle on us. The habits of our heart—spiritual exercises, practices, and other expressions of love—will flow naturally from our interaction with Him.

The writer of Hebrews summarized best what this book has been trying to say: "Let us fix our eyes on Jesus, the author and perfecter of our faith, who for the joy set before him endured the cross, scorning its shame, and sat down at the right hand of the throne of God" (Heb. 12:2). Let's fix our eyes on Christ, rendezvous with Him daily, and let Him make us like himself. God bless you in your love life with Christ!

NOTES

1. Written and contributed by Richard E. Buckner, ministry resources product line editor, Beacon Hill Press of Kansas City.

2. Bernard of Clairvaux, *On the Love of God,* quoted in *Devotional Classics: Selected Readings for Individuals and Groups,* ed. Richard J. Foster and James Bryan Smith (San Francisco: HarperSanFrancisco, 1993), 41-42.

3. Julian of Norwich, *Revelations of Divine Love,* trans. Elizabeth Spearing (London: Penguin Books, 1998), 49.

4. Gregory of Nyssa, *The Life of Moses,* trans., introd., and notes Abraham J. Malherbe and Everett Ferguson; pref. John Meyendorff, *The Classics of Western Spirituality* (Mahwah, N.J.: Paulist Press, 1978), 137.

5. Thomas à Kempis, *The Imitation of Christ,* quoted in *Spiritual Classics: Selected Readings for Individuals and Groups on the Twelve Spiritual Disciplines,* ed. Richard J. Foster and Emilie Griffin (San Francisco: HarperSanFrancisco, 2000), 150.

6. André Louf, *Teach Us to Pray: Learning a Little About God,* quoted in *Spiritual Classics,* 33.

7. Madame Guyon, *Experiencing the Depths of Jesus Christ,* quoted in *Devotional Classics,* 321.

8. Augustine of Hippo, "Our Lord's Sermon on the Mount," in *Augustin: Sermon on the Mount, Harmony of the Gospels, Homilies on the Gospels,* ed. Philip Schaff, vol. 6, *Nicene and Post-Nicene Fathers* (n.p.: Christian Literature Publishing Company, 1888; reprint, Peabody, Mass.: Hendrickson Publishers, 1994), 47.

9. John Wesley, "Letter to a Member of the Society, June 17, 1774," in *The Works of John Wesley,* 3d ed., ed. Thomas Jackson (1872; reprint, Peabody, Mass.: Hendrickson Publishers, Inc., 1984), 12:295.

10. Isaac Penington, *Letters on Spiritual Virtues,* quoted in *Devotional Classics,* 238.

11. Thomas à Kempis, *The Imitation of Christ,* trans. Stephen MacKenna (1896; reprint, London: Watkins Publishing, 2006), 140.

12. C. S. Lewis, *Mere Christianity* (New York: Macmillan, 1952), 167.

13. Teresa of Ávila, *Interior Castle,* quoted in *Devotional Classics,* 198.

14. Penington, *Letters on Spiritual Virtues,* 238.

15. Charles Wesley, "Help Us to Help Each Other, Lord," in *Wesley Hymns,* comp. Ken Bible (Kansas City: Lillenas Publishing Co., 1982), 110.

16. Dietrich Bonhoeffer, *Life Together,* trans. John W. Doberstein (San Francisco: HarperSanFrancisco, 1954), 106.

17. John Wesley, *A Plain Account of Christian Perfection* (London: Wesleyan Conference Office, 1872; reprint, Kansas City: Beacon Hill Press of Kansas City, 1966), 101.

18. Bonhoeffer, *Life Together,* 21.

19. John Wesley, "The Law Established Through Faith," in *Works of John Wesley* 5:455.

20. *Manual,* Church of the Nazarene, 2005-9, par. 27.

21. Charles Wesley, *Wesley Hymns,* 99.

22. Dietrich Bonhoeffer, *The Cost of Discipleship* (1937; 2d ed., SCM Press, 1959; paperback ed., New York: Macmillan, 1963), 86.

23. Hannah Whitall Smith, *The Christian's Secret of a Happy Life* (Uhrichsville, Ohio: Barbour and Company, 1985), 195-96.

24. Bonhoeffer, *Cost of Discipleship,* 101.

INDEX